PISCES
20 FEBRUARY – 20 MARCH

First published in Great Britain 2011
by Mills & Boon, an imprint of Harlequin (UK) Limited,
Eton House, 18-24 Paradise Road, Richmond, Surrey TW9 1SR

Copyright © Dadhichi Toth 2011

ISBN: 978 0 263 89662 6

Design by Jo Yuen Graphic Design
Typeset by KDW DESIGNS

Harlequin (UK) policy is to use papers that are natural, renewable and recyclable products and made from wood grown in sustainable forests. The logging and manufacturing processes conform to the legal environmental regulations of the country of origin.

Printed and bound in Spain
by Blackprint CPI, Barcelona

Dedicated to

The Light of Intuition

Sri V. Krishnaswamy—mentor and friend

With thanks to

Joram and Isaac

Special thanks to

Nyle Cruz for

initial creative layouts and ongoing support

ABOUT DADHICHI

Dadhichi is one of Australia's foremost astrologers and is frequently seen on television and in other media. He has the unique ability to draw from complex astrological theory to provide clear, easily understandable advice and insights for people who want to know what their futures may hold.

In the 26 years that Dadhichi has been practising astrology, face reading and other esoteric studies, he has conducted over 10,000 consultations. His clients include celebrities, political and diplomatic figures, and media and corporate identities from all over the world.

Dadhichi's unique blend of astrology and face reading helps people fulfil their true potential. His extensive experience practising Western astrology is complemented by his research into the theory and practice of Eastern forms of astrology.

Dadhichi has been a guest on many Australian television shows, and several of his political and worldwide forecasts have proved uncannily accurate. He appears regularly on Australian television networks and is a columnist for online and offline Australian publications.

His websites—www.dadhichi.com and www.facereader. com—attract hundreds of thousands of visitors each month, and offer a wide variety of features, helpful information and services.

MESSAGE FROM
◎ DADHICHI ◎

Hello once again and welcome to your 2012 horoscope book!

Can you believe it's already 2012? Time flies by so quickly and now here we are in this fateful year, a time for which several religions of the world—including the Mayans from 3100BC—have predicted some extraordinary events that are supposedly going to affect us all!

Some people are worried there will be a physical cataclysm that will kill millions and millions. Some are of the opinion it is the end of the economic and social models we have lived by for thousands of years. Others seem to believe the Planet Nibiru will whiz by planet Earth and beam up the 144,000 Chosen Ones.

Whatever the opinion, it is an undeniable fact that we are experiencing some remarkable worldwide changes due to global warming (even though that remains a point of contention) and other societal shifts. Scientific knowledge continues to outrun our ability to keep up with it, and time appears to be moving faster and faster.

But my own research has categorically led me to repeat: 'Relax, everyone; it is *not* the end of the world!' There will most certainly be a backlash at some point by Mother Earth at the gross unconsciousness of many of us. There will be ravaging storms, earthquakes and other meteorological phenomena that will shake the Earth, hopefully waking up those of us still in a deep sleep, dreaming, or possibly even sleepwalking. It is time to open our eyes and take responsibility.

If there are any significant global changes I foresee, they are the emergence of wider self-government and the greater Aquarian qualities of the coming New Age. This period is the cusp or changeover between the Age of Pisces, the Fish, and the Age of Aquarius, the Dawn of Higher Mankind.

Astrology, and these small books I write about it, are for the sole purpose of shedding light on our higher selves, alerting us to the need to evolve, step up to the plate, and assume responsibility for our thoughts, words and deeds, individually and collectively. The processes of karma are ripe now as we see the Earth's changes shouting to us about our past mistakes as a civilisation.

I hope you gain some deeper insight into yourself through these writings. For the 2012 series I have extended the topics and focused more on relationships. It is only through having a clear perception of our responsibility towards others that we can live the principles of astrology and karma to reach our own self-actualisation, both as individuals and as a race.

I hope you see the light of truth within yourself and that these words will act as a pointer in your ongoing search.

All the best for 2012.

Your Astrologer,

www.dadhichi.com
dadhichitoth@gmail.com
Tel: +61 (0) 413 124 809

◎ CONTENTS ◎

⊚ CONTENTS ⊚

CONTENTS
CONTINUED

PISCES
PROFILE

THE STATE OF YOUR LIFE IS
NOTHING MORE THAN A
REFLECTION OF YOUR STATE OF
MIND.

Wayne Dyer

PISCES SNAPSHOT

Key Life Phrase		I Sacrifice
Zodiac Totem		The Fish
Zodiac Symbol		♓
Zodiac Facts		Twelfth sign of the zodiac; mutable, fruitful, feminine and moist
Zodiac Element		Water
Key Characteristics		Loving, sensitive, intuitive, spiritual, idealistic, victimised and moody
Compatible Star Signs		Aries, Taurus, Cancer, Scorpio, Sagittarius, Capricorn and Pisces
Mismatched Signs		Gemini, Leo, Virgo, Libra and Aquarius
Ruling Planets		Jupiter and Neptune

Love Planets	❤	Moon and Mercury
Finance Planets	💲	Mars and Saturn
Speculation Planet		Moon
Career Planets	👤	Sun and Jupiter
Spiritual and Karmic Planets	🪷	Moon, Mars and Pluto
Friendship Planets		Saturn
Destiny Planet		Moon
Famous Pisceans	★★	Bruce Willis, Kurt Russell, Seal, Jon Bon Jovi, Albert Einstein, Victor Hugo, Aaron Eckhart, Drew Barrymore, Jessica Biel, Eva Mendes, Rachel Weisz, Dakota Fanning and Jean Harlow
Lucky Numbers and Significant Years		2, 3, 9, 11, 12, 18, 20, 21, 27, 29, 30, 36, 38, 45, 47, 48, 54, 56, 57, 74, 75, 81, 83 and 84
Lucky Gems		Yellow sapphire, gold, topaz, red coral and pearl

Lucky Fragrances	Rosemary, peppermint, black pepper, bergamot and ylang ylang
Affirmation/ Mantra	I offer my love to all but I am grounded
Lucky Days	Monday, Tuesday, Thursday and Sunday

◎ PISCES OVERVIEW ◎

When we look at the personality of Pisces, we see that your zodiac totem, the two Fish swimming in different directions, is no accident. The Fish reside in the ocean, which is representative of the emotional, sensitive nature of your star sign. The two directions represent your mind, which is often at odds with itself. Which way to go? is the question that occupies you in both your material and emotional lives.

Fortunately, being born under the twelfth sign—the final stage of the zodiac—endows you with insight and a gift for understanding everything at the deepest spiritual level. Although the Fish swim in different directions, and the ocean of emotions adds considerable turbulence to your life, you are anchored within yourself by this special grace, and you are now nearing the end of your evolutionary phase.

There are aspects of your personality that are not easy to understand, and others are sometimes at a loss when trying to figure you out. You don't consider yourself secretive, but because people are often unable to gauge the depth of your personality, they mistakenly assume that you do harbour secrets.

Once others get to know you, they will realise that emotion rather than reasoning rules your life. You base your decisions on your instincts, not your intellectual deductions. You are not a person of strong willpower preferring to go with the flow and daydream rather than practically implementing some of your ideas.

Idealistic Pisces

You are an idealist through and through, and love the idea of being in love. You are malleable and adaptable because Pisces is a mutable sign. You love to adjust yourself to different circumstances, and one could even go so far as to say that you like to wear different masks for different occasions.

You are loving and caring by nature, and you truly understand the meaning of unconditional love. You love to give yourself to others, and your compassion and understanding is coupled with your gentle and kind affection for one and all.

You are impartial in the way you live your life, so there are times when you become a victim of unscrupulous people who would take advantage of your generosity and goodwill. Learn to be less impressionable, and look more carefully at human nature in an unbiased fashion.

You have a wonderful ability to express yourself artistically due to your imaginative and sensitive nature. You are able to channel otherworldly ideas into your paintings, music and poetry. In fact, anything you do will have the touch of the mystical imprinted on it.

You understand people through your psychic abilities, but you must be careful not to get caught up with the people whose energies you absorb and whose lives you try to improve and save. In the end, you may become a victim of the very people you are trying to help.

One of the difficulties with your sensitive nature is that you avoid making hard decisions, especially if you feel it is going to undermine someone else. You'll do anything to help close friends and family members, but don't forget to help yourself. Some Pisces are so habituated to this attitude that they end up becoming the sacrificial lamb in their relationships. You should try to recognise when you're being used, because no one gains from this. Balancing your needs against those of others is a particularly important lesson for you during the course of your life.

INTUITION VERSUS RATIONALISM

Because you're an intuitive person, you don't always think through your problems thoroughly. Using your emotions and your deeper intuitive powers is the way you prefer to resolve life's challenges, even if others don't quite see the sense in that. Pisces, you are somewhat of a daydreamer, aren't you?

Your instincts are powerful and, more often than not, they are correct. Your ability to foresee an event before it actually happens is quite uncanny. I've known many Pisceans who are psychics and clairvoyants because they have the ability to act as mediums. Remember, though, that intuition can only go so far. Learn to develop your thinking processes as well as your intuitive feelings.

PISCES CUSPS

ARE YOU A CUSP BABY?

Being born on the changeover of two star signs means you have the qualities of both. Sometimes you don't know whether you're Arthur or Martha, as they say! Some of my clients can't quite figure out if they are indeed their own star sign, or the one before, or after. This is to be expected because being born on the borderline means you take on aspects of both. The following outlines give an overview of the subtle effects of these cusp dates and how they affect your personality quite significantly.

Pisces-Aquarius Cusp

If you were born between the 19th and the 25th of February, you were born on the cusp of Aquarius and Pisces. This means you partake of some of the elements and personality traits of each star sign. Aquarius is a forward-thinking and unconventional sign, so your intuitive and mystical qualities are blended with the avant-garde characteristics of the Aquarian temperament.

You have the ability to take traditional ideas and mould them into concepts that can be useful on an individual level or a group basis. Working in humanitarian and spiritual organisations—even hospitals—will give you the opportunity to express freely your natural inclinations in this Aquarius-Pisces combination.

Because you are born with a mixture of air and water, you sometimes find it difficult to balance the intellectual and emotional sides of your nature. Making decisions can be hard because you are prone to basing them on your gut feelings. You know full well that you need to rationalise some things and use your head, but you find this approach to be hard at times. You also find yourself thinking about how you feel, or feeling about how you think, and this kind of dilemma often becomes too much for you.

The typical Pisces is a daydreamer, so it's good that the intellectual and communicative aspects of Aquarius are enmeshed in your Piscean blood. This gives a more down-to-earth and expressive quality to the way you interact with others.

Being born with this blend of astrological signs is a blessing, and gives you a special sort of destiny. You are a true helper, an intuitive healer, and are able to soothe the wounds of friends and people generally. Your destiny will make you sought after as a truly unconditional lover and friend.

Pisces-Aries Cusp

If you are born between the 16th and the 20th of March, you draw in some of the fiery energies of the next zodiac sign to yours, Aries. This makes you a bolder sort of Piscean, with a mixture of the elements of water and fire. While the typical Pisces can sometimes be withdrawn and indecisive about which direction to take, the fire of Aries will make you more decisive, and even sometimes aggressive in your approach.

Because you are primarily concerned with helping others and giving assistance to those less fortunate than yourself, the strong ego of Aries will make it hard for you to balance yourself with others. There are times when you are swinging between sheer egotism and pure selflessness. For many of you, balancing these extremes will be a lifelong challenge.

You have a creative and enterprising nature, and want to achieve something in the world, but can also bring to your activities some wonderful spiritual and emotional qualities.

You must temper your ambitions—your emotionalism can cause you to work too hard, and you may, at some point, suffer the consequences through physical illness. Once again, if you are able to balance your driving needs with your moments of emotional intensity, you have a great chance of becoming successful and fulfilling yourself, both out in the world, and within your own being.

PISCES CELEBRITIES

FAMOUS MALE:
DANIEL CRAIG

Daniel Craig was born Daniel Wroughton Craig on the 2nd of March, 1968, in Chester, England. Daniel has become a world-renowned actor, making his name as a rugged on-screen personality. Although ruggedness doesn't usually represent the Piscean temperament, in Daniel we can see the malleability of the Pisces individual. I mentioned earlier how Pisces can assume different masks for different occasions. He's the perfect example of how Pisces is able to don the garb of any character that is required of them.

Daniel began his profession in theatre, and eventually went on to star as James Bond in *Casino Royale* in 2006 and *Quantum of Solace* in 2008. The high-tension scenes in these films are some of the most memorable.

The idealism of Pisces can be seen in Daniel's approach to his career. There have been times when he turned down well-paying jobs in favour of work that was in keeping with his emotional and spiritual needs. He honed his craft in a series of art-house and European productions, and chose to do mainstream projects only when he felt that the parts were perfect for him.

That Daniel is highly respected in his craft is shown by the fact that he was snapped up to star alongside Tom Hanks and Paul Newman in *Road to Perdition*. He has even been chosen by Steven Spielberg to star in some of his work.

FAMOUS FEMALE:
EVA MENDES

Eva Mendes, the sultry on-screen actress, was born on the 5th of March, 1974, in Houston, Texas. When Eva was very young, her parents moved to Los Angeles. She's the youngest girl of four children, having two sisters and one brother.

Eva comes from a down-to-earth middle-class family. Her father worked as a meat distributor, while her mother was a bank teller.

From an early age, she dreamed, as most Pisces-born natives do, of achieving something wonderful in her life. But she probably thought that a miracle would be needed to get her out of the circumstances she was in. In her own words, she confesses that ever since she was a young girl, she desired the luxury of the high life and to be rich, because she saw just how poor her family was.

Eva aspired to become famous because of her poor background, but she also developed her compassionate side. She was honoured at an annual Power of Women luncheon in Los Angeles, along with six other stars, for her humanitarian efforts. Compassion and selfless service are some of the most dominant character traits of Pisces.

She graduated from Hoover High School and decided to study marketing at California State University, Northridge. Had she not become an actress, she may have gone on to do interior decoration. But as a means of earning some extra money, Eva decided to appear in a small feature film.

As a result of this, a photographer neighbour took some snapshots of her at a garage sale, and placed them in his portfolio. Later, an agent noticed Eva's photos and asked to meet her. It was at this meeting that the agent asked her to quit school and take on a career in acting.

Some of her famous films include the blockbuster *2 Fast 2 Furious, The Women, The Other Guys* and *All About the Benjamins* with Ice Cube. In 2003, when she starred with Denzel Washington in the film *Out of Time*, her popularity started to soar. Playing alongside Will Smith in the romantic comedy *Hitch* didn't hurt her professional prospects either. Eva has continued to woo audiences worldwide, and will continue to be a popular on-screen star.

PISCES

AT LARGE

LEARN FROM YESTERDAY, LIVE FOR TODAY, HOPE FOR TOMORROW.

Albert Einstein

⊚ PISCES MAN ⊚

♂

PISCES MAN:
SNAPSHOT

Self-sacrificing

Romantic

Insightful

Creative

Hyper-sensitive

Those of you born under Pisces have few, if any, prejudices. People must understand that you're not primarily motivated by what you can get out of life, but by what you can give. Although you are not ambitious (in the strict sense of the word) for status, fame or fortune, you still aspire to achieve something notable, and if wonderful things come to you, that's all well and good. However, your main focus is on helping others and making a difference.

You are a dreamer of the highest order, but you need to be careful not to let these dreams cloud your practical judgement of things. You must crawl before you can walk by focusing on just one thing every now and again, because you have a great knowledge of many subjects and may even be an expert in a few of them. As a result, you are at risk of dispersing your energy in a scattered fashion, just like your totem, the two Fish constantly swimming in different directions.

You are a person of the people: you are impartial and never look down on anyone. You are equally comfortable with a beggar or a king, and your intuitive responses to life's situations make you sought after by one and all for your unbiased advice.

Piscean men are usually quite emotional and moody underneath, but somehow manage to exude a happy and carefree attitude. People love your company, and you are a social creature by nature.

Although you love stability in life, you tend to be on the move, seeking out new adventures and possibly even romantic partners. You have such high aspirations that you are sometimes let down. Later in life, you will realise that maybe you placed too much faith in people who, in the end, were simply there to use you for your good nature.

You oscillate between being a socialite and a hermit. If you are not happy or don't feel well, you don't want to impose these emotions on others, tending to stay alone and keep to yourself at these times.

Your memory is very powerful, but you must be careful to filter out all the negative events that are going to weigh you down in the present and the future. Think only of the good things, and this will help make your path that much easier.

You have the ability to embellish the truth. This is due, in part, to the rulership of Pisces by Jupiter. Jupiter is the largest planet and has a reputation for exaggeration. Coupled with your co-ruler, Neptune, this exaggeration can take the form of lies. You must be careful not to detour from the truth.

People are fascinated by your uncanny ability to understand them so easily. It's as if, when they meet you, they feel you've known them all their life. In the middle of telling them about their personal tribulations, they'll catch themselves out and ask: 'Why am I telling you all this?' The reason is simple, Pisces. You have the ability to draw people out of themselves because of your compassionate and understanding nature. Is it any wonder why many of you become counsellors, healers, nurses and aides? You just have that natural ease and approachability that people trust. A word of advice, though: never take advantage of others under these circumstances.

You're a free person who wants to explore life on your own terms, so if rules and regulations start to hem you in, you are likely to buck at authority. You need complete control over how and when you do things, and if you're in a circumstance where regimentation is high on the agenda, you'll find it difficult to be happy and stick with it.

There are moments when you are slightly lazy and can't be bothered with things. It's at these times that you need to find ways to motivate yourself to remain focused on the goals you set for yourself. And when people obstruct you, they might get to see the aggressive, stubborn side of your personality. It's not a good look. Try to control this with the spiritual composure of which you are so very capable.

PISCES WOMAN

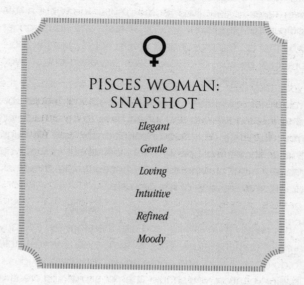

PISCES WOMAN: SNAPSHOT

Elegant

Gentle

Loving

Intuitive

Refined

Moody

If you are born under Pisces, you are indeed blessed—Piscean women are elegant to the core. Being a gentle and sensitive creature, you are ruled by the planet Neptune, which governs the oceans. Your feelings, your depth and your grace are just as deep as the sea and often as unfathomable, even to those who know you well.

You're fundamentally a kind and loving person, and this is what others love about you. You don't really have to use words: your presence and your beautiful eyes say it all. You are the quintessential combination of the sensual and the mystical. Pisces, incidentally, is a feminine sign, and it symbolises your femininity completely.

You're a dreamer, a visionary. Piscean women have wonderful imaginations that need to be expressed in every area of their lives. Some of your ideas are a little difficult for people to accept at first, and you wonder why that is. You must admit you're not always the most practical person, and your ideas are often out of sync with current trends.

You're also extremely romantic, which is why any person who falls in love with you would have to be considered most fortunate. You love unconditionally, and although this is something people often talk about doing, you make a point of living this way because it is an actual, practical expression of who you are.

You have an amazing aptitude for seeing into things more deeply than others, and can therefore tap into any area of human nature. This, in turn, means you're able to do original work and come up with progressive ideas. In your vocation, you should attempt something creative because you really do produce dazzling works of art.

The surprising outcome of your keen insight into human nature is that you're very idealistic about people. You take people at face value, and are very honest in the way you deal with them.

You're not altogether motivated by money, but this doesn't mean you won't achieve your goals financially—if that's what you choose to do. You see money as a form of energy, a direct reflection of the time and love you put into doing a good job. Generally, however, you like to help others in some way, therefore, you don't always feel comfortable doing a job based on self-interest. You like to help the downtrodden, and are comfortable looking after friends and strangers alike.

Piscean women are quite sociable, and because artistic refinement is part of their personalities, combining creativity with fun appeals to you. Because you understand the inherent beauty in yourself and others, you're attuned to nature, and are respectful of the majesty of life and the universal mind.

You have particularly strong family ties, which are vitally important to you. You need to have a close-knit family. The hub of family life gives you the opportunity to make yourself available if and when you're needed. To you, support for your family is a lifelong commitment. Many Piscean women take on a caring role for sick or ailing relatives as they become older.

Head-on confrontation is something you avoid like the plague. You don't like to get involved in clashes with others. If you have to deal with someone who's antagonistic, you'll put up a wall rather than sort out the problem. You need to work on this to resolve issues in your most personal relationships. Don't let apathy or weakness overcome your ability to be an emotionally strong being.

It's best for Pisces to remain active and not be too preoccupied with negative thoughts. Alcohol and drugs are best avoided, even in moderate amounts, because it's too easy for you to become hooked on addictive substances.

☙ PISCES CHILD ☙

If your child is a Pisces, for the most part you, can expect them to be caring, loving and sensitive. But while these words might best describe your child, but they are by no means exhaustive in revealing the complexity of people born under the sign of the Fish. Even as a youngster, the eyes of your Pisces child will reflect the wisdom with which they've been born.

From an early age, their bright and seductive eyes, and their awareness and understanding of others, are quite surprising. You probably have no problem believing that they have been reborn because it's as if they've brought their knowledge from somewhere else. Even if they don't use language, they have the unique ability to speak to you through their eyes, with a gesture or a casual glance.

Working on a routine of discipline will be hard if you're a parent of a Piscean child, because they're so sensitive. They are likely to withdraw when you try to impose rules and regulations on them. If you punish them, they'll possibly make you feel guilty for doing so, but you mustn't give in—simply discipline them in a gentle fashion. Parents should stick to certain codes of conduct so their little Pisceans grow into balanced and well-adjusted adults. Again, don't mete out heavy-handed punishment to them—they need to see you're being fair and loving in your discipline.

Your Piscean child is very artistic, and you'll see that their music or painting skills are well in advance of their years. You ought to encourage them in any way you can, and you'll often hear their teachers refer to them as naturals. They love artistic activities and are happiest when they are painting, singing or dancing.

Pisces and Selfless Sharing

Pisces children are always ready to share whatever they have. They also enjoy their parents sharing in their activities with them. You can build a wonderfully loving parent-child relationship through sharing time creatively with them.

Piscean children, being water signs, love swimming and getting involved in any water sports. These will bring out the best in them because their totem, the Fish, lives in the ocean. It makes sense to teach them how to swim very early, because that way, they will get the joy of playing in water, as well as the exercise they require.

Exercise is essential for your Pisces child because they have the tendency to put on a few kilos as they start growing older. A regime of physical exercise will help keep that in check. Make sure they have a good schedule of movement and physical activity, which will encourage them to develop it into a habit they continue throughout their lives.

Pisces children love pets. They're very loving and nurturing when they play with animals, and will make their pet their best friend. This is the foundation for many Piscean children becoming carers in the greater community later in their lives.

PISCES LOVER

Pisces-born individuals are somewhat vulnerable in love. They give themselves so easily, so fully and so unconditionally to their partners that they often overlook studying those with whom they fall in love. Because you are so unreserved and non-judgemental in your love, Pisces, we might even refer to you as the perfect lover of the zodiac. You've always dreamt of love and the ideals of perfection, but you need to make sure you're going to be fulfilled in a relationship. The reality of love is often not in keeping with your vision of it. However, you don't believe love is an impossible dream, so you never give up the goal of finding your perfect soulmate.

Sensitive Pisces

Pisceans are fragile and susceptible, so it is imperative that those becoming involved with them treat them with the utmost respect and sensitivity. If you hurt a Piscean through deception or infidelity, it is hard for them to recover, and they will carry that pain for a long time.

Pisces need a lot of love and acceptance, and because they are so giving, they really need the same the sort of responses from their partner. They need a companion who is going to stimulate them and trigger their imagination—in terms of everyday communication as well as in the bedroom. Water signs, such as Pisces, know how to nurture and protect their partners. This is because they are ruled by the element that governs the emotions.

You want to give yourself so completely to the one, Pisces, you love that you often become oblivious to the other aspects of life. You mustn't become blinded by your emotions. However, when your soulmate, your true love, comes into view, you'll see this as the turning point in your life. You'll give your all to satisfy them. Even if your partner is not necessarily unconditional (as you are), you'll still be happy to give them your love whole-heartedly. You hope that they will also, in time, be able to give you greater satisfaction. Don't smother your lover. You must give them enough space to develop their own interests, and they'll appreciate this gesture.

You know how to keep romance alive by making it interesting. You're innovative in the way you show your affection, and can keep the flames of passion burning bright into old age, if you so choose. You often think up different ways of expressing your love, and this is what maintains your partner's interest. Sentimentality is a strong part of your character. You cry at the drop of a hat. When a friend has a problem or suffers a tragedy, you feel as if this is your own problem and will share in their suffering.

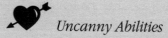

Uncanny Abilities

One of the uncanniest abilities of Pisces stems from your intuitive skills: you are so in tune with your lover that you always know what is going on in their mind and heart. When they have a problem, you are aware of it. You are a step ahead in helping them solve their problems, much to their surprise and appreciation.

If, like some Pisceans, you are on a never-ending treadmill looking for love, you will find your emotions are not fulfilled. The danger for Pisceans is that the reality of love forever falls short of their imaginary, perfect lover. As I've said before, you must keep your desires realistic and your assessment of others real.

Sexually, you must have a partner who will give in return. For you, physical intimacy is an extension of your personality, and you love to give of yourself whole-heartedly. Venus and Libra are the planet and sign of your relationships, respectively, and they regulate the sexuality of Pisces. You therefore have a natural connection with sex and physical intimacy. If you happen to meet the right person, you'll totally surrender yourself and enjoy the lovemaking that ensues.

Your partner will appreciate your caring and considerate behaviour. Just don't overdo your open-handedness. Don't become too needy, or your partner will lose respect for you. You're deeply committed to long-term, stable relationships, and you seek the security of a family environment to do your job as a parent. You instinctively understand the nature of unconditional love, and this is where, as a parent, you excel. Raising children will be one of the most satisfying experiences for you, Pisces, because you were definitely born to love.

⊙ PISCES FRIEND ⊙

As a friend, you are extremely loyal and understanding. This is, first and foremost, what draws others to you in their search for friendship.

Once you make a friend, you like to keep them for a long time. You tend to become very emotionally attached to them, and speaking again of your unconditional love, you mustn't ignore those times when others are taking advantage of you. It's one thing to be a friend, but you mustn't be a fool. Stand up for yourself, because self-respect is an essential ingredient of a two-way friendship.

You love the social interaction of friendship and a good dose of humour. These components are what you believe make up a healthy relationship. You are a great listener and love to ponder the problems of others—it is in this domain that you can show your love and care by helping your friends work through their issues.

Loving, Loyal Pisces

Being sensitive and humane are some of the other traits that endear you to others, and give you a reasonably good circle of friends. Loyalty is the jewel in your crown, and you look to your friends to be just as caring as you are.

You enjoy spending time alone as much as you love partying, because Pisces has a spiritual dimension to its connections, including those to yourself. You often look to the spiritual potential of your friends and this will sometimes take them aback. On the one hand, they see you are comfortable with groups of people in party situations, while on the other, you can be like a hermit. Balance these two sides of your nature, or at least explain to your friends what is going on so they can gain a greater understanding of you.

With your friends, you like sharing creative and imaginative activities. You see this as a way of drawing friends closer to one another. You want to do things that are interesting, off-beat and generate creative impulses, not just in yourself, but in your social group. You love seeing your buddies excel emotionally, artistically and spiritually.

Being friends with a Pisces is a multi-dimensional experience, and requires a broad mind and big heart to reciprocate the love they offer.

☉ PISCES ENEMY ☉

Piscean Grudges

You need to understand that Pisceans are, essentially, emotional beings, and once they have been mistreated, they don't easily forget what has happened. They never quite trust someone who has hurt them, and they hold on to their feelings for a long time. Although they are able to forgive, they don't easily forget.

Pisces, you sometimes believe that you are *never* at fault. Your ego can get the better of you, and this sets you up against others. It's at this point that people will turn on you, and even if they are the ones at fault, you need to deal with blame in a diplomatic fashion so that friendships and workplace relations don't deteriorate any further. Acknowledge when you are wrong.

If you have made an enemy of someone and they offer you an apology, you must learn to accept it. Another ingrained trait of Pisces is that, although you are forgiving, you find it hard to accept apologies. And sometimes when your faults are pointed out, you prefer to ignore the observation and pretend they don't exist. You must accept that you aren't perfect, and accept constructive criticism. This will most certainly help you avoid making enemies.

PISCES
AT HOME

IT MAY BE HARD FOR AN EGG TO TURN
INTO A BIRD: IT WOULD BE A JOLLY
SIGHT HARDER FOR A BIRD TO LEARN
TO FLY WHILE REMAINING AN EGG. WE
ARE LIKE EGGS AT PRESENT. AND YOU
CANNOT GO ON INDEFINITELY BEING
JUST AN ORDINARY, DECENT EGG. WE
MUST BE HATCHED OR GO BAD.

C.S. Lewis

☙ HOME FRONT ☙

Pisceans have a wonderful imagination and often live in a fantasy world, so it's only natural that their homes reflect this. Your home is your safe haven in which you can express many of the fantastic ideas that you usually can't in the outside world.

You want to live freely within your domain, and like to express yourself whenever and however you please. Because routine is something you don't often adhere to, you oscillate between bouts of extreme cleanliness and wanton untidiness.

Because you are social, inviting friends and relatives over to partake of your fantasy world is something you love to do. In this context, you share your feelings and your love through different activities and gestures. Your home is often the central point of socialising with your peer group.

Pisces also rules such things as monastic life, which is why, at the other end of the spectrum, you often prefer to be completely alone, shunning the world. Home represents your private paradise where you can connect with otherworldly energies and channel these vibrations into your personal realm.

Mood lighting and other artistic objects will feature strongly in your domestic sphere. You have an eclectic style, and your furniture mixes different periods to create a rather unusual—and certainly not boring—visual experience for visitors to your home.

Candles, mirrors, photography and, in particular, artworks that utilise soft watercolours are features that reflect your personality perfectly.

You have a high degree of sentimentality and nostalgia enmeshed in your personality, which is why you like to keep mementoes of friends and family close at hand. It's not unusual, when visiting the home of a Pisces, to see photographs of family members in unique picture frames.

Gifts, floral arrangements and candles with unusual scents are all part of the mix in the home environment of a Pisces. These sensual stimulants range from simple pieces to foreign and exotic items that remind you of the many experiences of your life.

HOME IS A TEMPLE

Because Pisces is a spiritual and artistic sign, they exhibit furnishings and accessories such as indigenous statues of gods and goddesses, sticks of incense, and music to match. Many Pisces' homes exude the energy of a temple. You like to make others not only feel at home, but want them to take something away once they've visited you, even going so far as to believe that you can affect their spiritual evolution in some way.

Finally, it wouldn't be too crazy to point out that Pisces, which has the totem of the Fish, could be inclined to include a tank containing multi-coloured tropical fish in their homes. This would provide a living contrast to the other furnishings of your unique dwelling.

Creating fantasy is important to you. You want your house to reflect your idealism, dreams and artistic nature.

KARMA, LUCK AND MEDITATION

Pisces represents the final stage in the soul's evolution, meaning you are on the last leg of your karmic journey, so to speak. Exploring the available spiritual possibilities comes naturally to you, and your main motivation for living is to discover your higher self, and to express that in your life.

The ruling star sign of your past karma and good fortune is Scorpio, which indicates your intense drive to explore the truth. Scorpio is one of the most psychic of the signs, which is why you are endowed with an abundance of intuition. One of your major karmic lessons will be to balance your spiritual gifts with a practical attitude. Sometimes this is hard for you, however, because you spend far too much time giving yourself to others and not focusing on the practicalities of your own life.

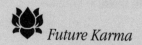

Future Karma

Your future karma is ruled by the sign of Cancer and the Moon. This tells us that your future is bound up in your emotional and spiritual life, because Cancer regulates feelings and intuitive responses. It also shows that good karma will come to you as a result of nurturing and caring for others in a selfless manner.

'I Sacrifice' is your personal life phrase, and this means you will make speedy spiritual progress by offering your best to others. You mustn't, however, take this as some sort of negative mantra, becoming a victim to every man and his dog who seeks help from you. The counterbalance to your life phrase is 'I am discriminative'.

Because you're so emotional, it is imperative that you spend a little time each day calming yourself and meditating on higher ideals. By doing this, you will be in a better position to deal with the day-to-day grind, and not get carried away by the demands of everyone around you. If you can do this, you will find the perfect balance between the world of spirit and the world of everyday responsibilities.

Lucky Days

Your luckiest days are Monday, Tuesday, Thursday and Sunday.

Lucky Numbers

Lucky numbers for Pisces include the following. You may wish to experiment with these in lotteries and other games of chance:

9, 18, 27, 36, 45, 54, 63

2, 11, 20, 29, 38, 47, 56

7, 16, 25, 34, 43, 52, 61

Destiny Years

The most significant years in your life are likely to be 3, 12, 21, 25, 30, 34, 48, 52, 57, 66, 75 and 84.

HEALTH, WELLBEING
◎ AND DIET ◎

Your ruling element is that of water, and this has a marked influence on your emotions and relationships. There is now clear evidence that much of people's physical health rests on their emotional and mental wellbeing. The interrelatedness of these things cannot be denied. For you, Pisces, it is even more important because you are so sensitive by nature. If you don't manage these aspects of your personality, you will start to find your physical wellbeing quickly deteriorating.

You must take full responsibility for your health by realising that how you experience each and every moment in the present is slowly impacting on the quality of your health over the long term. Make sure you have a regular routine in your work. Set aside enough time for exercise and recreation, and sleep and eating, as this will help maintain your health. You mustn't oversleep or undersleep. Six to eight hours is perfect for you, and will help increase your vitality.

Pisces rules the feet, toes and toenails. It also rules the lymphatic system, and the subtle or astral circulation system through which your life force passes. Perform Hatha yoga or other aerobic exercise that includes flexible stretching. This will make your muscles supple and improve your circulation while calming your emotions. Learn to relax as much as possible, because this will assist in removing self-defeating thought patterns. In turn, this will further increase your health and wellbeing.

Some Pisceans eat way too much as a way of coping with emotional problems. You mustn't eat to suppress your feelings. If you reduce your food intake, your health will improve dramatically. By keeping active, you will maintain regular digestion. Vitamins A, B and magnesium are important for your health. Try eating lots of fruit and vegetables, particularly broccoli, celery, green peppers, tomatoes and cherries.

Soy bean products, bean sprouts, eggs and sunflower seeds are great additions to your diet. Because your lower extremities—like your feet and ankles—can be a problem for you, supplement your diet with Vitamin B complex, plus beans and legumes.

⊚ FINANCE FINESSE ⊚

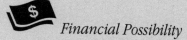

Financial Possibility

Pisces individuals are not overly preoccupied with making money, but when they put their minds to it, they can acquire a small fortune. Aries and the planet Mars dominate the second zone of Pisces, which governs the moneymaking sphere of your life. Once you decide to earn money, you can do it with great energy and creativity, as shown by the personality of Mars.

Take care with managing your money, because while Mars shows you can earn well, you have a tendency to be impulsive in the way you spend it. Being an argumentative planet also indicates times throughout your life where money will become a sticking point in your relationships. It is always a good idea to discuss financial matters, and to reach an agreement on them before moving forward with someone in a partnership. This will then help you avoid any subsequent financial misunderstandings.

It's interesting to note that Capricorn rules your sector of business profitability, for this is a rather conservative and thrifty sign. This indicates that once you have your head out of the clouds and your feet firmly planted on the ground, you can make some headway in your moneymaking ventures.

PISCES

AT WORK

THERE IS MORE TO LIFE THAN
SIMPLY INCREASING ITS SPEED.

Mahatma Gandhi

◎ PISCES CAREER ◎

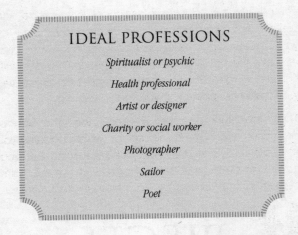

IDEAL PROFESSIONS

Spiritualist or psychic

Health professional

Artist or designer

Charity or social worker

Photographer

Sailor

Poet

You are quite changeable, Pisces, so you may find it difficult to choose a professional path and stick to it. You're strongly motivated to pursue a career, but sometimes you aren't sure what you want to spend your life doing. Take some time, do the research, and try to find the vocation that best suits your temperament.

Because Pisces is an emotional sign, you should do work that gives you satisfaction on this level. Also, your caring nature needs to express itself through what you do. You want to do something that serves others. If you feel that you're helping, you'll be satisfied. All of this indicates working with people.

In the way you work with other people, you have a sense of fair play. This is what your co-workers love about you. You're a hard worker, and don't believe that you have a right to anything, but that you are responsible for the good that comes to you.

The helping and healing professions, such as social and welfare work, nursing and dietetics, would be ideal for you. Pisceans also make excellent teachers, so the path of education could be worth investigating. Working with children or people with mental or physical disabilities would also be fulfilling for you.

There are other possible directions, too. The sign of Sagittarius rules your career sector, which indicates you have a love of variety, travel and general learning. And your ruling planet, Neptune, hints at careers in television, film, photography, art, music, dance and other creative areas.

Sun

You have a lot of energy and drive in your approach to work, which is shown by the Sun and Leo ruling your workplace arena. Because the Sun is your willpower and drive, and is associated with your sixth zone of selfless service, you are excellent in health-related careers, social work and other services engaging with the general public.

Jupiter

Jupiter, your career ruler, governs mobility, teaching and spiritual pursuits. Even if you don't pursue a career as a spiritual leader or philosopher, you will have a sense of ethics in the way you conduct yourself professionally. Your honesty and integrity are powerful accessories to the skills you bring to your work.

❂ PISCES BOSS ❂

Although your Pisces employer sometimes prefers to be alone rather than dealing with too many people, he or she is still an approachable person—they are considerate, understanding and fair in their dealings with others. You know they will be honest with you, and won't knowingly take advantage of anyone.

As a water sign, a Pisces employer will be rather moody and temperamental and, as a result, you may not know quite what to expect from them when you turn up at the office every day. Will he be happy, or will she be sad? This will certainly keep you on your toes. You might have to develop the same level of intuition as your Pisces boss in order to understand exactly where they are emotionally from one moment to the next.

One thing about your Pisces boss is that he or she will always take the time to make sure you're happy in your personal life. They understand that a happy and well-integrated employee is beneficial to the company. In this respect, the Pisces employer is always considerate of the welfare of their employees—to them it is not always about money. The bottom line isn't the bottom line with a Pisces boss.

Empathy and consideration, coupled with an unconventional creative mind make working for a Pisces boss an experience in itself. But you mustn't be afraid of sharing your opinions with them, especially if you see them getting distracted or off-course. They'll appreciate your attention because they need a little guidance here and there, even though they are the one in charge.

Pressure is not something that the Pisces boss handles all that well, and when the going gets tough, making decisions can make things even harder. Under pressure, their anxiety sets in, and the Pisces imagination can get the better of them. They always tend to worry about the worst situation: 'Will there be enough money to get through the month?' and so on, and so forth. You should encourage them, and let them know that you're as loyal to them as they are to you.

You must understand, if you're being interviewed for a job by a Pisces, that they have excellent powers of perception and intuition, and are a judge of character second to none. So don't try to pull the wool over their eyes and pretend to be something you're not. If you don't have the requisite skills or training, it's best to be upfront and honest with them, because they will respect this much more than if you fake it.

⊚ PISCES EMPLOYEE ⊚

Working with a Pisces employee requires delicate handling, particularly if you are an employer. Bringing out the best in your Pisces colleague needs refined understanding and sensitivity.

Pisces workers are full of imagination, and need your support in allowing them to express this in their job. If this is not possible, you will soon see a rather depressed, lazy and apathetic individual—they need an adequate outlet for the subtle energies of their personality.

But although the Pisces employee needs freedom to feel comfortable at work, you must monitor this. They do need some boundaries and direction so their creativity doesn't become scattered and unproductive. With an accomplished, guiding hand, you'll be able to bring out the best in them, and eventually feel confident enough to give them the autonomy they so desire.

Enthusiastic Employee

As long as your Pisces employee enjoys their work and feels creative in it, you shouldn't have too much trouble getting them to perform well. If the position involves serving others, rendering assistance or giving advice, then rest assured they will do an excellent job and feel fulfilled at the same time.

There are times when personal pressures get the better of Pisces, so if you see them detached and antisocial, you'll know that something is wrong. Generally, they mix well with others at the office, so being withdrawn is a telltale sign that you need to take them aside and counsel them to find out what is wrong. There's nothing worse than having a Piscean employee who is overwhelmed by personal problems. This will radically affect their performance on the job.

PISCES AND MONEY

You'd be mistaken if you thought that money was the main motivator for a Pisces employee. They need more than that. A sense of belonging, an appreciation for what they do and the opportunity to help others take pride of place for them.

Your Pisces employee is a friendly co-worker who is loyal, hardworking and shrewd in the way they conduct themselves. There are times where you'll be caught off guard because they don't seem all that ambitious. But while money isn't their main motivation, this is not to say they aren't ambitious. Many Pisceans bide their time, and are quite capable of heading up large organisations after paying their dues.

PROFESSIONAL RELATIONSHIPS: BEST AND WORST

BEST PAIRING:
PISCES AND CAPRICORN

Capricorn falls in the zone of financial profitability for you, a sector of the zodiac that is also considered a zone of friendship for Pisces. Because of this, the two of you can create a commercial arrangement that is profitable, and all the while enjoy good camaraderie as part of the financial association.

You are indeed lucky if you have Capricorn as a financial partner. Although your governing planets are not particularly friendly, the elements of water and earth tend to function well together, and the opposing forces of your ruling planets can assist in uplifting each other, equalising your energies, and bringing stability to the business association.

Capricorn is frugal, conservative, determined and ambitious to achieve good results in their business enterprises. You will appreciate these traits, and will not have anything to worry about when they take control of the financial aspects of your partnership. Capricorn will feel comfortable knowing that you bring to the business your imagination and wonderful sensitivity for people. A mutual respect will underpin your relationship, which is why this is an excellent match in business.

Capricorn doesn't have much time for your emotionalism or occasional bad moods. If they find that this is starting to interfere with the smooth functioning of the business, they will tell you (in no uncertain terms) how they feel. But the way in which they do this will be a benefit to you, and can help you grow as an individual. You have a great deal of respect for your Capricorn partner, knowing that they have the inbuilt wiring to sniff out a good deal, and the commercial maturity to teach you how to become a better businessperson. With your Capricorn partner, you will learn a lot and develop your skills professionally.

There are times when Capricorn becomes very serious about work and life. These are where you can counterbalance their rather sombre and dragged moods by showing them that life is not all about money and materialism, but can include spirituality, too. By giving them this sort of balance, they will grow to respect and love you, as well as appreciate what you bring to the business. This is an excellent match that should be prosperous and fulfilling for both Pisces and Capricorn.

WORST PAIRING:
PISCES AND VIRGO

Why would you bother getting into a business relationship with Virgo, knowing full well how rational and critical they are? You observed this at the outset of meeting them, did you not?

The reality is that Virgo is dominated by its ruling planet, Mercury, which is completely preoccupied with analysis, attention to detail and practical issues. Yes, the earth element of Virgo indicates they will keep things on an even keel, but even so, with Virgo you feel as if you have very little scope to exercise your imagination and spiritual idealism in your commercial relationship. You, on the other hand, have the spiritual planets of Jupiter and Neptune governing your life and activities. These planets are essentially enemies of Mercury. The way they function is very, very different to one another, and they reflect the dysfunctional interaction between the two of you.

Although you are both motivated by the principle of selfless service, Virgo's approach is poles apart from yours. You have a spontaneous attitude and like to do things from the heart, relying on your instincts more than anything else. Even if your head tells you that something is not exactly right, you prefer to give more weight to your intuitive assessment of the person or situation, and then act.

This just won't do with Virgo, who will spend huge amounts of time questioning, reasoning, deducting and generally driving you crazy. You will see this as a criticism of your way of organising business, assessing whether people are right for the job, and so on. On this one point—which is, I might add, no small matter—you and Virgo will just not draw the same conclusions. Time and time again, you will disagree, and this will affect the viability of your business. I might even go so far as to say that it could become an astrological hell for both of you.

You'll become impatient with Virgo because of their desire to make sure that everything is right, perfect, and in keeping with their pristine values. You too like to see the perfection in things, but not in the same way as Virgo. You tend to believe that doing things as best as you can, as long as your heart is in the right place, is, in itself, a form of perfection. Virgo's notion of perfection can be reduced to a very simple one-plus-one-equals-two equation.

You are not all that motivated by money, but Virgo has a strong sense of economy. So when it comes to keeping the books, you will also find yourselves at loggerheads. In the end, you will probably give full control of the finances to Virgo simply to keep the peace, which is also a very important thing to you.

When all is said and done, I can say that a business relationship with Virgo will be more work than it's worth. If you're going to spend this much effort working through the relationship itself, then you'll hardly have time to focus on where your energies are most needed: in the business itself.

PISCES

IN LOVE

IT'S NOT THE MEN IN MY LIFE THAT
COUNT; IT'S THE LIFE IN MY MEN.

Mae West

ROMANTIC
◎ COMPATIBILITY ◎

How compatible are you with your current partner, lover or friend? Did you know that astrology can reveal a whole new level of understanding between people, simply by looking at their star sign and that of their partner? I'd like to share some special insights that will help you better appreciate your strengths and challenges using Sun sign compatibility.

The Sun reflects your drive, willpower and personality. The essential qualities of two star signs blend like two pure colours that produce an entirely new colour. Relationships, similarly, produce their own emotional colours when two people interact. The following section is a general guide to your romantic prospects with others and how, by knowing the astrological 'colour' of each other, the art of love can help you create a masterpiece.

Each of the twelve star signs has a greater or lesser affinity with the others. The two quick-reference tables will show you who's hot and who's not as far as your relationships are concerned.

The Star Sign Compatibility table rates your chance as a percentage of general compatibility, while the Horoscope Compatibility table summarises the reasons why. The results of each star sign combination are also listed.

When reading I ask you to remember that no two star signs are ever *totally* incompatible. With effort and compromise, even the most difficult astrological matches can work. Don't close your mind to the full range of life's possibilities! Learning about each other and ourselves is the most important facet of astrology.

Good luck in your search for love, and may the stars shine upon you in 2012!

STAR SIGN COMPATIBILITY FOR LOVE AND FRIENDSHIP (PERCENTAGES)

	Aries	Taurus	Gemini	Cancer	Leo	Virgo	Libra	Scorpio	Sagittarius	Capricorn	Aquarius	Pisces
Aries	60	65	65	65	90	45	70	80	90	50	55	65
Taurus	60	70	70	80	70	90	75	85	50	95	80	85
Gemini	70	70	75	60	80	75	90	60	75	50	90	50
Cancer	65	80	60	75	70	75	60	95	55	45	70	90
Leo	90	70	80	70	85	75	65	75	95	45	70	75
Virgo	45	90	75	75	75	70	80	85	70	95	50	70
Libra	70	75	90	60	65	80	80	85	80	85	95	50
Scorpio	80	85	60	95	75	85	85	90	80	65	60	95
Sagittarius	90	50	75	55	95	70	80	85	85	55	60	75
Capricorn	50	95	50	45	45	95	85	65	55	85	70	85
Aquarius	55	80	90	70	70	50	95	60	60	70	80	55
Pisces	65	85	50	90	75	70	50	95	75	85	55	80

In the compatibility table above please note that some compatibilities have seemingly contradictory ratings. Why you ask? Well, remember that no two people experience the relationship in exactly the same way. For one person a relationship may be more advantageous, more supportive than for the other. Sometimes one gains more than the other partner and therefore the compatibility rating will be higher for them.

HOROSCOPE COMPATIBILITY FOR PISCES

Pisces with		Romance/Sexual
Aries		You love Aries unconditionally and fulfil them sexually; the two of you have powerful sexual urges
Taurus		Taurus is sensual and understands the way you enjoy lovemaking—this can be an excellent match
Gemini		Gemini lives in the realm of the mind and you find this totally disconnecting sexually
Cancer		You have a common bond in your emotional and intuitive feelings—excellent romantic combination

	Friendship		Professional
✔	On a one-to-one, level you can be great friends, but your social activities may differ vastly	✘	You may be far too easygoing for Aries' strong-willed nature; financially, you may be too lax for them
✔	You are very well suited in the astrological scheme, and make great friends	✔	There are fine opportunities for a steady business involvement Taurus
✘	The way you live your lives is very different, and you are both changeable	✘	Not a great financial combination—both of you may be too scattered for anything of lasting value
✔	You're very attracted to each other as friends, so this relationship really is quite unique	✔	This is a mutually supportive relationship that will satisfy you both, and has excellent long-term prospects

Pisces with		Romance/Sexual
Leo		Your emotional and sexual connection is not run of the mill, but by the same token, it is not all that bad, either
Virgo		You fully express yourselves sexually but this is quite a challenging relationship
Libra		Because of the strong Venus connection, this match *may* have something going for it, but it is turbulent as well
Scorpio		It will be easy to build a relationship, and Scorpio offers you comfort and undying loyalty

Friendship	Professional
✘ Leo will help you develop your self-esteem, especially if you are the shy and retiring type of Piscean	✔ Because of your gentle and loving support, Leo will see this as an asset professionally
✘ Pisces and Virgo relationships are usually contradictory on a friendship level—not great	✘ Virgo has the brainpower to run the business; stick to the imaginative side of the deal and this could work
✔ Librans love socialising and will constantly entertain you, but give them their freedom	✘ Idealistically, this is not the best of matches, although your personalities could come together commercially
✔ Both of you understand and aspire to the deeper, emotional sides of life	✔ Excellent business combination, just don't let excessive emotions drag you down

Pisces with		Romance/Sexual
Sagittarius		A sexually loving and nurturing existence and children will be your mutual goal
Capricorn		Capricorn will appreciate your patient ways; a loving and mutually supportive relationship is indicated
Aquarius		Physical intimacy is a powerful attractor between you, blending emotions and intellect
Pisces		This will be a mutual relationship of undying love

Friendship	Professional
✔ There's a great alignment between Pisces and Sagittarius, therefore friendship is excellent	✘ This business partnership needs dialogue to get on the same page about money
✔ Opposite character traits often attract, so you may find something appealing in each other as friends	✔ Capricorn has a great capacity for sustained work, and being a wonderful and selfless worker yourself, you will benefit them
✘ Get Aquarius to reveal what they want so you can see whether or not the two of you have enough similarity in your goals	✔ You might think Aquarians are unusual intellectual types, but your business life with them will never be boring
✔ You're both concerned with sacrifice and serving others, so be careful you don't become victims of your own ideals	✘ You must clearly try to establish the nature of your business alliance if you are to have a long-term partnership

PISCES
◎ PARTNERSHIPS ◎

Pisces + Aries

You can love Aries unconditionally because that is your intrinsic nature. You'll be able to fulfil Aries' sexual appetite, too, because both of you have powerful urges. Aries will reciprocate sexually, but they mustn't take your kind nature for granted.

Pisces + Taurus

Initially, there will be challenges associated with faith and trust, but these are two lessons you will learn from each other if you choose to make a go of this partnership. Taurus will bring you down-to-earth and help you gain a greater understanding of practical, day-to-day affairs. This might be hard for you to accomplish at first, but if anyone can teach you, it is Taurus.

Pisces + Gemini

Once you get to know Gemini, you'll see they are not that superficial after all, and actually have a great deal of insight. Once you connect on this level, then the true sharing in this relationship will start. Spend some quiet time together to allow your different personalities to get to know each other. By doing this, you'll learn to see beyond the superficialities of Geminis, and will soon understand that there is good potential for you with them.

 ### Pisces + Cancer

Fortunately, you have a common bond in your emotional and intuitive feelings. You understand Cancer's moody character and, even if they hold on to grudges for way too long, you will both forgive and forget your misunderstandings very easily and move on. Remember Pisces, you too can be moody!

 ### Pisces + Leo

Pisces thinks of things beyond their own immediate needs. You are very selfless and compassionate this way. You are unselfish and motivated by seeing other people happy. Leo, on the other hand, likes to feel socially and materially satisfied through their ego. What motivates you is really quite different, and this will be a hard thing to reconcile. But if there is respect and tolerance for each other's differences, this combination can move forward.

Pisces + Virgo

Pisces and Virgo relationships are contradictory on every level. Even though opposite signs are traditionally considered positive for love, romance and marriage, you are both such different people in your approach to life that it is hard to see this working for you. You will need to dig deeply, and find common ground in other areas of your lives to fulfil each other.

 Pisces + Libra

You prefer listening to talking, and if they don't accept this, your approach to communication will frustrate Libra. Sometimes Libra talks for the sake of talking, and this irritates you because you have no problem with silence as a means of communication. Pisces is well aware that silence is the subtlest language of love.

 Pisces + Scorpio

Magic can and will happen in a combination of Pisces with Scorpio. It's one of those remarkable unions often referred to by astrologers. These two water signs bring out powerful emotions and sentiments between them, resulting in an overwhelming and uninhibited passion.

Pisces + Sagittarius

Sagittarius is such a fiery and outgoing sign that they will push your easygoing personality to a point where you might retaliate—but know that you mustn't. Because you're flexible, use that ability to adjust to them and learn how you, too, can be more animated. Take the initiative to achieve your dreams. Even though you don't like being pushed, there are lessons you will learn from Sagittarius.

Pisces + Capricorn

You feel with your heart, not your mind, because you are the supreme daydreamer. Capricorns just can't get their heads around this. They need to know there is a practical and ambitious facet to your nature, or they might just walk. This will be driven home if you get into a long-term relationship because Capricorns need security above all else. But strangely, this relationship can still work.

Pisces + Aquarius

Aquarius will bring out and reveal aspects of your past that bother you. They may also be people whom you've known in the past. They will draw to the surface the emotional aspects of your character for you to deal with and remove from your life. A remarkable change will take place for you personally by being involved with them.

Pisces + Pisces

You have a sublime love for each other, and will surrender yourselves to the cause of love. For both of you, this might seem like a supernatural, mystical experience. As Scorpio and Cancer, the other two water signs, you will have a truly wonderful relationship with Pisces. This will be a relationship of undying love.

PLATONIC RELATIONSHIPS: BEST AND WORST

BEST PAIRING: PISCES AND TAURUS

Pisces and Taurus have an awful lot in common. Even though you are a water sign and Taurus is an earth sign, you somehow manage to feel comfortable in each other's company.

Sometimes a difference in the quality of the elements of star signs is quite essential for a relationship to be balanced, with a counteraction of two kinds of energy occurring. In Taurus, you can't go past them for being grounded—this is their unique strength. If you ever wanted someone to help pull your head out of the clouds, then Taurus is the perfect choice. As you know, friends should be there for each other, and the one thing you will experience with your Taurus companion is their unflinching loyalty, their persistence and devotion to an ideal. You greatly appreciate this.

When you find yourself floating off, mystically daydreaming about this, that or the other, Taurus will always be there to bring you back to Earth, and get you to question your motives and aspirations. Taurus will pose such questions to you as: 'Are you being practical enough about this? Will it serve you in the future? Is this the best way to get around the problem?'

Taurus is straightforward in many respects. They are very different to you, in that you are a complex individual who likes to look at life and its meaning from different perspectives. Your main thrust is to understand life and get to know what makes it tick. This doesn't mean that your Taurus friend will distract you from investigating and discovering the mysteries of existence, but they will always question you as to the viability and practicality of your activities. I would have to say that your friendship with Taurus will greatly help your practical evolution.

Taurus individuals are sometimes a little slow off the mark, and they can be mistaken for snobs and people who just don't know how to have fun. Because you are patient, however, you will discover that Taurus can open you up to a whole gamut of experiences, entertainment and cultural activities. You will enjoy this part of your friendship with them.

WORST PAIRING: PISCES AND LEO

You tend to think of things beyond your own immediate personal needs, and this is due to the fact that Pisces is selfless in every sense of the word. This is not something you need to cultivate—your spiritual attitudes seem to be genetically hardwired into your personality.

In a friendship with Leo, you might feel as if you are doing all the giving and not receiving anything in return. This may sound like a contradiction, because you take such pleasure in giving of yourself unconditionally, don't you? Hey, Pisces, there's a limit to everyone's saintliness, and you are no exception.

For a time, you may find it quite novel to support Leo's bravado and endless need for the limelight, but after a while, you'll ask yourself, 'What's in it for me?' Leo tends to be quite self-absorbed, and you might wonder whether they have any time or energy for you. This will start to play on your self-confidence. The last thing you want to do is become a victim, but this is often what happens to Pisces when they hitch themselves to people who take advantage of them.

One of your main lessons with Leo, if you choose to befriend them and spend time together, is to learn tolerance for each other's differences. If that's possible—and not just a one-way street with you doing all the work—then the relationship may have a slight opportunity of moving forward. But you can see it will be an uphill battle.

Leo is a fixed sign, so their opinions are sometimes inflexible. You will find it difficult to express yourself with someone who has to be right all the time. The trouble is that your planets are quite friendly astrologically, but the underlying tension sees you circling around the same difficulties continuously.

You have a strong need for fantasy, to explore the unknown, and you do this in a gentle, emotional manner.

Your association with Leo may unsettle the approach that you prefer to take with life. At the end of the day, you may find it extraordinarily difficult to reconcile your differences with the showy Leo.

SEXUAL RELATIONSHIPS: BEST AND WORST

BEST PAIRING: PISCES AND SCORPIO

There is truly a magical quality between the star signs of Pisces and Scorpio, and there are very few astrologers (if any, that I can recollect), who would advise against a relationship between you.

The beauty of this combination lies in the fact that, as well as being elementally perfect for each other, Scorpio is the ninth sign to yours, indicating strong and unavoidable karmic connections. When you meet your Scorpio partner, it's as if the forces of nature take over—you will be unable to stop the destiny that fate has carved out for you.

Being water signs means you are emotionally sensitive, and the two of you will immediately connect on this level. Your feeling nature is so highly developed that you appreciate the same level of sensitivity in your Scorpio partner.

Both of you will meet each other's needs perfectly, and this is, therefore, a great match. A combination of Pisces and Scorpio is ideal, with Scorpio being able to understand your intuitive needs. You know how to touch them in body, mind and spirit. When you work your way into each other's hearts, you are going to fall head over heels in love.

Each of you has the ability to understand the deeper, more emotional sides of life. As a consequence, you're able to open your hearts to each other and share feelings that others are often unable to express.

Again, the ninth sign reveals what you are destined to do. Scorpio has the ability to help you understand this. As well as a strong sexual and emotional connection, your spiritual ideals should generally move along the same pathway. This is, therefore, going to create a very special attachment between you. Scorpio is soothed by your presence, and their inner passion and intense reactions are calmed by your compassionate personality. You both feel tranquil in each other's company, like a still lake.

Some Scorpios carry an intense past with them, and seek love and understanding from someone who can release them from these turbulent feelings. You are the perfect person for this and will help balance their life. Once the two of you have created this special connection, you'll find it hard to remain apart.

Both of you have strong intuitive powers, and when it comes to communicating ideas, it's as if you both understand exactly what the other is thinking. That goes a long way towards creating sexual satisfaction as well. Often in relationships, partners are out of sync with each other. In a relationship between Pisces and Scorpio, this is hardly ever a problem. You both instinctively feel when the other needs love and when to back off. This is a wonderful foundation for a long-lasting and fulfilling relationship at pretty much every level.

WORST PAIRING:
PISCES AND LIBRA

Transposing your sexual ideals onto those of a Libran is a recipe for disaster. You have extremely different perspectives on reality, and mixing those up in a sexual relationship won't give it a great chance of working. In fact, you may end up irritating each other, especially when you realise that Libra is such a social creature. You will soon discover that their sense of the domestic is a far cry from being satisfactory.

Librans are very indecisive. If you are a Piscean woman trying to make a go of it with a Libran male, you will become completely exasperated at the lack of leadership displayed by your counterpart. You need someone who is prepared to take responsibility, and you look forward to a fulfilling family life with children. In the early stages of Libra's life, they may not be at all partial to being tied down in this way.

Pisceans have such an idealistic view of love that once it is shattered, it is hard for them to reconnect with romance again. You dream of perfection, of unconditional love and selfless, spiritual idealism. In the first instance, Libra may appear to offer you this, but you'll soon realise that their flirtatious ways will betray you. But who knows, this could be the best thing to happen, especially early on in the piece, so you can move on and be with someone much more compatible.

When Libra realises you're not going to put up with their flighty social agenda, and you start asking for answers, they will interpret this as nagging. Here is where your real problems will begin. At this stage of the game, you'll probably find yourself hiding away in the comfort and security of your home, while Libra continues to seek social comforts outside the relationship. You will have to start rethinking your partnership. The danger is that you will retreat into a world of fantasy rather than accept that a Pisces and Libra match may not be all you thought it would. Remember, Pisces, there are plenty of fish in the sea, and being a fish yourself means it shouldn't be too hard for you to join another shoal.

In some of my previous work, I have spoken of the special connection between Venus, the ruler of Libra, and Pisces, in which Venus is exalted. Astrologically, this means there are ample opportunities for Libra to explore a relationship with Pisces and gain immensely from it. So I am not saying that an evolved Libran can't find fulfilment with Pisces, it's just that finding a Libran of such a progressive calibre to satisfy Pisces will be an almost impossible task.

QUIZ:
HAVE YOU FOUND
YOUR PERFECT
⑥ MATCH? ⑥

Do you dare take the following quiz to see just how good a lover you are? Remember, although the truth sometimes hurts, it's the only way to develop your relationship skills.

We are all searching for our soulmate: that idyllic romantic partner who will fulfil our wildest dreams of love and emotional security. Unfortunately, finding true love isn't easy. Sometimes, even when you are in a relationship, you can't help but wonder whether or not your partner is right for you. How can you possibly know?

It's essential to question your relationships and to work on ways that will improve your communication and overall happiness with your partner. It's also a good idea, when meeting someone new, to study their intentions and read between the lines. In the first instance, when your hormones are taking over, it's easy to get carried away and forget some of the basic principles of what makes for a great relationship that is going to endure.

You're probably wondering where to start. Are you in a relationship currently? Are you looking for love, but finding it difficult to choose between two or more people? Are you simply not able to meet someone? Well, there are some basic questions you can ask yourself to discover the truth of just how well suited you and your partner are for each other. If you don't have a partner at the moment, you might like to reflect on your previous relationships to improve your chances next time round.

The following quiz is a serious attempt to take an honest look at yourself and see whether or not your relationships are on track. Don't rush through the questionnaire, but think carefully about your practical day-to-day life and whether or not the relationship you are in genuinely fulfils your needs and the other person's needs. There's no point being in a relationship if you're gaining no satisfaction out of it.

Now, if you aren't completely satisfied with the results you get, don't give up! It's an opportunity for you to work at the relationship and to improve things. But you mustn't let your ego get in the road, because that's not going to get you anywhere.

Pisces are idealistic lovers who often make the mistake of falling in love with the wrong partner. Your idealism is sometimes blinded to the reality of the person before you. If you're already in a relationship, it's important to analyse how well suited you are to each other, and if things are not so good, how you can improve on them.

So here's a checklist for you, Pisces, to see if he or she's the right one for you.

Scoring System:

Yes = 1 point   No = 0 points

- ❓ Does your partner value your dreams?
- ❓ Does your partner care for you romantically?
- ❓ Is he or she sensitive to your feelings?
- ❓ Does your partner share your vision of having a child some day?
- ❓ Does your partner always reassure you that you are the only one?
- ❓ Does your partner always tell you that they love you?
- ❓ Does your partner remember important and sentimental dates, like when you first met?
- ❓ Does he or she value your opinion?
- ❓ Does your partner value your traditions?
- ❓ Does your partner give you time alone when you need it?
- ❓ Are you proud of your partner when you are introducing him or her to others?
- ❓ Do you visualise being with your partner in the future and always?

❓ Does your partner respect your intuition?

❓ When you are with your partner, do they make you laugh, and do they engage you in deep conversation?

❓ Is your partner loyal to you?

❓ Are you and your partner romantically and firmly attached to each other?

Have you jotted down your answers honestly? If you're finding it hard to come up with the correct answers, let your intuition help and try not to force them. Of course, there's no point pretending and turning a blind eye to treatment that is less than acceptable, otherwise you're not going to have a realistic appraisal of your prospects with your current love interest. Here are the possible points you can score.

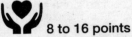 **8 to 16 points**

A good match. This shows you've obviously done something right, and that the partner you have understands you and is able to reciprocate in just the way you need. But this doesn't mean you should become lazy and not continue working on your relationship. There's always room to improve and make your already excellent relationship even better.

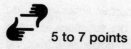

5 to 7 points

Half-hearted prospect. You're going to need to work hard at your relationship, and this will require a close self-examination of just who may be at fault. You know, it takes two to tango and it's more than likely a combination of both your attitudes is what is dragging down your relationship. Systematically go over each of the above questions and try to make a list of where you can improve. I guarantee that your relationship will improve if given some time and sincerity on your part. If, after a genuine effort of working at it, you find things still haven't improved, it may be time for you to rethink your future with this person.

0 to 4 points

On the rocks. I'm sorry to say that this relationship is not founded on a sufficiently strong enough base of mutual respect and understanding. It's likely that the two of you argue a lot, don't see eye to eye or, frankly, have completely different ideas of what sort of lifestyle and emotional needs you each have. The big question here is why are you still with this person?

Again, this requires some honest self-examination to see if there is some inherent insecurity which is causing you to hold on to something that has outgrown its use in your life. Old habits die hard, as they say, and you may also fear letting go of a relationship that you have become accustomed to, even though it doesn't fulfil your needs.

Self-honesty is the key here. At certain times in life you may need to make some rather big sacrifices to move on to a new phase, which will then hopefully attract the right sort of partner to you.

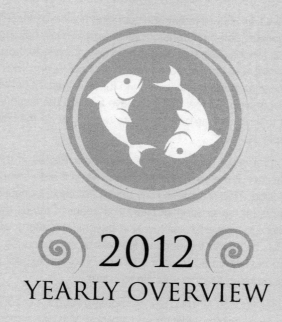

2012
YEARLY OVERVIEW

THINGS TURN OUT BEST FOR THOSE
WHO MAKE THE BEST OF THE WAY
THINGS
TURN OUT.

Jack Buck

⊚ KEY EXPERIENCES ⊚

For a while, Saturn remains in your eighth zone of shared resources, personal transformation and sexuality during 2012, Pisces. This has been an important cycle for you, and it is now coming to an end. You'll still spend most of the year giving consideration to these issues, but after October, you will feel that you have learned the lessons that this planet has been trying to teach you for the last couple of years.

Neptune, your ruling planet, hovers near Pisces in the early part of the year, until February, when it enters your Sun sign. This is a particularly significant cycle because this planet takes approximately 164 years to transit the zodiac. Its powerful spiritual and psychic vibrations will be felt by you in the coming few years, and because it is so closely linked to your star sign, you can expect a major turning point in your life to occur.

Jupiter, your other ruling planet, moves through your zone of travels, communication and siblings. You can expect these areas of your life to be considerably affected by its impact on your horoscope. This is a positive influence, and will bring you good luck in these areas. You also have some favourable opportunities associated with contracts, verbal agreements and anything related to education this year.

ROMANCE AND
◉ FRIENDSHIP ◉

You are particularly fired up this, year and Mars will see to it that love and romance are high on your agenda. Unfortunately, you need to be careful that you don't misdirect your energies and turn your passion into conflict. Mars is notorious for provocation, and being in your zone of relationships means the first half of the year should be spent with you treading carefully in matters of love.

SEXUALITY AND PISCES IN 2012

Saturn does not augur well as far as your sexual intimacy is concerned, and it may put the brakes on your physical expression of love. I have mentioned that you will be passionate, but this aspect of your horoscope means you'll be experiencing a tug-of-war between the physical and the emotional aspects of your relationships.

Your partner may not want to talk to you as much, which might lead you to believe they have lost interest in you, or that you're not good enough for them. As a result, your self-confidence may start to wane. However, during this type of cycle, it is imperative you open the door to communication so that any issues can be dealt with in the most transparent way possible.

With Pluto transiting your zone of friendships, you will feel an intensity in this area of your life as well. As the year commences, the Moon and Pluto show that one or two friends may be demanding your attention, and jealousy, emotional games or blackmail may create problems in your relationships. You must use the excellent energies of Jupiter to communicate and negotiate a truce.

Venus, of course, is extremely important in assessing the strengths and benefits you are likely to experience in your romantic and marital life. In February, Venus brings with it loads of opportunities to express your love and to receive it in return. Once again, when Venus transits your zone of romance in August and September, you can look forward to having fun times and passionate interludes with the one you are with now, or perhaps even with a new lover.

 Relationships on the Rise

With Venus in your zone of secrets and secret spiritual activities, you'll want to stay away from the world and rediscover the simple things that once made you happy. The trick is to experience happiness in the hustle and bustle of your daily grind. This means your relationships could be low-key, or you and your partner might prefer to spend time away from the social crowd for the first few weeks of the year.

After the 23rd of January, you will want to enjoy relationships again, but may also want your freedom. Can you have it both ways? Perhaps you should be looking for freedom within your relationship. In other words, if the person you are with is open-minded enough, they will allow you your independence, and to conduct yourself in ways that are in keeping with your nature. That is what having a true soulmate should be about.

Your relationships seem to be on a seesaw after the 14th of March, when Mars and Venus are in a favourable aspect. You will need to keep a balanced view of things if you are to understand your partner's needs. For example, you may wish for something a little more unusual, for more spice in your life, for variety that your partner may not be able to offer you just now.

Discussions centre on love and relationships as Mercury enters your fifth zone of love affairs on the 7th of June. You are ready to open up and explore the possibilities of your romantic nature. This may be difficult when you're feeling private and perhaps even a little suspicious, given some of the things that have happened in the past. I always say that the most fragrant rose has the thorniest stem, and the prick of the thorn is the price you pay for the rapturous heights of love.

....

CREATIVITY IN 2012

After the 3rd of July, Mars activates your creative energies. This is the perfect time to investigate the sorts of things you can do to bring yourself back to a level of expressive brilliance so that you can love more completely.

....

Venus and Mercury give you a jolt after the 7th of August. Your heart may be telling you one thing, while your head challenges you and tells you to hold back. You may be relying on your store of good karma to get you through this period, but remember, you're only as good as your last hit, as they say in the music industry. Travel is high on your agenda, and this should trigger an interest in spiritual destinations.

Your emotional intensity is not met by your spouse or partner around the 4th of October. You won't understand why they're not as excited about a topic or lifestyle that you are dreaming about. How can you bridge the gap between your vision and theirs? This is the vital question.

WILD IN NOVEMBER

By the 17th of November, the wilder side of your nature is likely to come out, so be careful—others may not understand you. You can't be all things to all people. And you will still need to respect convention in certain circumstances.

WORK AND MONEY

Harness Your Moneymaking Powers

Making money can be summed up in an equation:

$$m \text{ (\$ money)} = e \text{ (energy)} \times t \text{ (time)} \times l \text{ (love)}$$

If one of the above factors is not present—for example, energy or love—you could still make money, but you won't be ideally fulfilled in the process.

It's absolutely essential to understand the universal laws of attraction and success when speaking about money. It is also necessary to understand that when you love what you do, you infuse your work with the qualities of attention, love and perfection.

With these qualities, you endow your work with a sort of electromagnetic appeal: a power that draws people to your work and causes them to appreciate what you do. This, in turn, generates a desire for people to use your services, buy your products and respect you for the great work you perform. This will without a doubt elevate you to higher and higher positions because you will be regarded as someone who exercises great diligence and skill in your actions.

This year, the position of Uranus promises to bring a great deal of innovation to the way you work and earn money, Pisces. From the outset, you will be wired for finance.

You're purposeful in gaining some concessions in a contract or agreement after the 14th of March. These energies will continue to get stronger until some clear and decisive action is taken after the 14th of April.

The lunar eclipse on the 4th of June in your zone of career and self-esteem reveals that you need to pay more attention to the currents of public opinion and what's happening in the world so that you understand your place contextually. You may think that what's going on has nothing to do with you right now, but actually, it's a perfect reflection of what is happening with your own being. This eclipse will have important ramifications for your professional activities from here on.

Mars has a strong part to play with regards to finance, and on the 3rd of July, its entry into your zone of shared resources, banking and legacies means that these issues will come to the fore. You must be careful you don't become embroiled in disputes over money or who owes what to whom.

CONTRACTS AND AGREEMENTS

You can be successful in signing contracts in March and April. From the 14th of March, you become much clearer on your goals, and have the energy and self-confidence to ask your superiors for exactly what you want.

Jupiter is an important finance planet and also governs your emotional achievements. Its retrograde movement on the 4th of October indicates that your career activities could be thrown into a tailspin. You need to manage your time and efforts very carefully after this date.

Pay special attention to real estate matters after the lunar eclipse on the 29th of November. There will be prime opportunities to invest money or, if you are the owner of an investment property, the chance arises to sell and make some fast money.

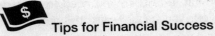 **Tips for Financial Success**

Innovation is the key word for the planet that most obviously influences your finances throughout 2012. Uranus has just nudged into your zone of money, earnings and material values. From the first week of January, with the Moon lending its support, you will be excited about the prospect of earning well in the coming twelve months.

All things modern and forward-thinking will be connected to the way you earn as a result of Uranus dictating your affairs. You'll start to see results as early as the 8th of January, when Mercury enters your zone of profits.

Because of your warm nature and compassionate works, don't be surprised to find that you're being recognised for your good deeds. There may be some positive press going around about you, and you'll hear pleasing things up to the 17th of February. If you are asked to act, you should do so before the 12th of March, when Mercury goes retrograde, creating havoc in some areas of your business life.

After the 17th of July, you must not vacillate between sheer brute force and killing others with sweetness. Which of these do you think is going to work? As the Buddha wisely said, perhaps the middle road would be most useful. Then again, you may still need force in some situations, and kindness in others.

Allow your intuition to guide you in matters of work, and don't be dictated by others' thoughts. After the 7th of October, your way is clear to achieve an important position in your company, or to seek a completely new job altogether. Your hard work will eventually pay off.

ECLIPSE HIGHLIGHT

An important eclipse occurs on the 14th of November, pointing to where you can invest or least understand how to create more money. In the case of Pisces, real estate and other fixed assets—along with strong connections to your family—are key to this understanding.

After the 11th of November, when Mercury positively enhances your profession, you will hear good news, or will petition for a new position.

 Career Moves and Promotions

If you have an ideal, or a passion for some creative activity, you mustn't feel unable to share this with others. Practise with one or two close friends first, especially if you trust them and know their criticism will be constructive. There are indications that you can capitalise on some hidden talent after the 25th of February. The first stage is to investigate, the second to activate, and the third to initiate.

When Mars and Jupiter favourably influence you around the 14th of March, your ideas and presentations will be met with respect and goodwill. If you're looking to secure a new job, this is an excellent time to think big and expect the best for yourself. Financial opportunities will also present themselves.

Mars transiting eighth house on the 3rd of July prods you to move up a gear if you're in a competitive arena and want that job. You may have to be ruthless to achieve greater financial benefits. You mustn't feel disadvantaged by others. Take full responsibility for your current position, and do what you can to change it.

If you're not enjoying your work, this may be impacting on your health. As hard as it is, you must start loving what you're doing so that, eventually, you'll be doing what you love. A career move could be initiated by the desire to improve your wellbeing and lifestyle. The period from the 4th to the 23rd of October is a time when you should consider these changes.

Career activities skyrocket after the 22nd of November, with an unusual job opportunity developing at this time. It could be related to what challenges you the most, but you'll get a thrill out of the contest and excel at everything you do at that time.

 When to Avoid Office Politics

Office politics seem to be part and parcel of work these days, so it's good to know when antagonistic, stressful days are going to ruffle your feathers.

Secret enemies may be discovered around the 21st of January. The start of the year is good for you professionally, but you may use up some of your time and emotional energy trying to focus on work rather than on the backstabbers.

Around the 16th of April, and then again after the 15th of July, the Sun in opposition shows that your responsibility and conscientiousness regarding the material aspects of life will be important. By stepping up to the plate and proving you can do this, you will provoke an immense amount of envy, so this is a time when office politics will abound.

Although, at first, this transit may be difficult for you to comprehend or execute, you will start to get the hang of it. You will see just how important it is to provide future security for yourself and your family, and to build a solid foundation of disciplined thinking and action. Ignore critical comments from the sidelines.

Around the 7th of September, be careful not to share too much private information with those who may use it against you. You'll be generous, and someone could take advantage of your open-handed nature. If you want to loan someone money, for example, make sure that you receive a promissory note. To avoid problems with co-workers, you need to have a clear set of guidelines up front.

The solar eclipse on 14th of November tells the story of potential legal and contractual issues. You may have to wrangle with red tape and manipulative individuals at this time. If you allow yourself to be drawn into the ego battles that are often found in the office, you'll waste an inordinate amount of time.

Around the 9th of December, you may suffer some sort of crisis, due to the fact that you're not able to release your tension. This could be caused by someone in your workplace giving you a hard time.

HEALTH, BEAUTY AND LIFESTYLE

 Venus Calendar for Beauty

Venus is not exactly one of your friendliest planets, so special attention should be given to it to highlight your best features and energies in 2012. Because Venus is in the sign of Aquarius as the year commences, you will need to rethink your image and the ways in which you project your personality. Beauty for you this year will be something very unusual, indeed, Pisces.

Some important Venus planetary aspects take place during 2012, and at these times, you should do your best to work harder on your makeup, clothing and accessories. You will feel completely comfortable in your own skin, and after the 14th of January, will feel Venus making you attractive to potential partners, and even to yourself. Your confidence is bolstered.

BODY CARE AND VENUS

Make an extra effort with your posture and, in particular, your footwear. Pisces is notorious for foot troubles. If, for example, you wear high heels, they could be impacting on your spine. Your wellbeing and health need to be looked at from a holistic point of view. From the 22nd of July until the 7th of September, work on your diet, and cleanse your skin more thoroughly for the best results.

On the 3rd of October, Venus moves to your zone of marriage, public relations and the world at large. You will be noticed at this time. Your beauty will lead you to some good fortune. This is also a good time for tying the knot in relationships. Once again, if you look great, you're more likely to have an offer of this sort come to you.

Venus and Jupiter promise good fortune through your wellbeing, and cause you to exude a clean and attractive aura after the 9th of November. Usually, this is attended with gifts, special privileges, or introductions to people who can further your profession or your social activities. Because you look good and feel great, people are more likely to be attracted to you, and will want to help you.

 Showing off Your Pisces Traits

Each zodiac sign has its own unique power based on the elements and planets that rule it. Unfortunately, most people don't know how to tap into this power and bring out their greatest potential to achieve success in life.

In the next twelve months, you have the perfect opportunity to show off your best traits due to the movement of your ruling planet, Neptune, in your Sun sign. This has not yet happened in your lifetime, so astrologically, it is quite significant. With this transit comes an activation of your most powerful Piscean instincts. Spirituality, in particular, will seem very natural to you. Your instincts (or, should I say, your intuition) will be so powerful that you immediately understand other people's intentions, even their thoughts. You should feel an acceleration of these energies after the first week of February.

With Venus transiting your Sun sign in January and February, you will find it much easier to express yourself, not just through the spoken word, but through gestures and subtle life forces. This is a difficult thing for me to explain, but let me assure you that you will know exactly what I mean once you start to feel these powerful undercurrents from your ruling planet, Jupiter, and from Venus. Venus again makes important contacts with your ruling planet on the 8th of March, the 16th of August, the 21st of September and the 9th of October. These are peak periods for your wellbeing and beauty. Use them wisely.

Some people are unaware of the ability for Pisceans to express themselves uniquely. This stems from their capacity to draw upon deep creative resources that are unavailable to others. During this cycle, you may surprise people by producing unusual, even incredibly original ideas, and your peers may not understand just how you are doing it. Much of this will take place between May and July.

Many of your Piscean traits and, in particular, those positive aspects of your personality that are destined to shine in 2012 will be triggered by the trend of Jupiter, your ruling planet. You will need to make special efforts when Jupiter moves retrograde in the early part of October. Observe your behaviour, diet, and any emotional patterns that affect your youthfulness and attractiveness generally.

Best Ways to Celebrate

When you celebrate your birthday, anniversary and other important events, it's important for friends and loved ones to understand that your Piscean temperament is partial to ethereal, exotic and spiritual themes, and to events that provide friends and family with something of a unique experience. Generally, Pisceans love to socialise and serve others while giving them a memorable experience.

Your lucky planet this year, Mars, excites you from its strong position in your marital zone. This area also has much to do with the public generally, and with people as a whole. Therefore, you will want to celebrate with crowds of people you love and trust. When the planets activate Mars in your seventh house, you will want to celebrate and generally have a great time. Some of the key dates surrounding these transits include the 23rd of August, the 1st of September and the 3rd of October (which is important because Venus also enters your marital zone at this time). During these cycles, expect some fun and fulfilling times.

Celebrations occur in June and July, and you can expect them to involve your family. If there are any past problems in your relationships, this is the time to let bygones be bygones, and to throw a party that can reconnect the dots of your family interactions. This will truly be a celebratory period.

....

PARTY WITH FRIENDS

Currently, you have an intense need to be with friends, to share your good fortune and happiness with them. This year, celebration will not simply be about having a great time drinking and partying, but more importantly, it will be about connecting with others and experiencing the joy of their happiness.

....

Your dreams can be fulfilled later in the year, especially between the 24th and the 31st of December, which is the usual festive season. However, something magical may also happen at this time. It will be something you don't quite expect, and it could have you jumping out of your skin!

KARMA, SPIRITUALITY AND EMOTIONAL ⊚ BALANCE ⊚

The most important planets regulating your spiritual and karmic destiny are the Moon and Mars. The future is determined, to a large extent, by the way you lived your past life, and you will now be experiencing the fruits of these actions.

In 2012, Mars, because it rules your past karma, tells us that much of your work will be in the area of friendships, marriage and other intimate relationships. Although this planet is a benefactor to you, it still exhibits its aggressive and sometimes dangerous energies, so you must be on guard not to repeat your past mistakes. In this way, you will direct the energies of Mars in a wholesome manner. You'll be challenged a great deal this year, especially up until Mars's exit from this extremely important zone of your horoscope in July.

Your good karma may be delayed as Mars moves retrograde on the 24th of January. Your patience will be tested, but if you flow with this transit, you will reach extraordinary spiritual heights and attain some good material benefits.

The lunar and solar eclipses have an influence on your future karma. On the 21st of May and the 4th of June, these eclipses aggravate your domestic and professional activities, and you'll be forced to choose a course of action at these times. Finding a balance may not be that easy.

As Mars returns to its karmic arena on the 24th of August, you will have special insights relating to your past. The solution to issues that have plagued you for a long time will come to light. Mars is a physical planet, so you can expect these benefits to be felt on the physical plane, resulting in increased energy and a feeling of wellbeing, mobility and lightness.

 Spiritual Highlights

In October and November, Mars will bring its basket of goodies to your career zone and then your social sector. In quick succession, you could feel the forces of nature carrying you along, so you can enjoy the benefits of your past good deeds in full measure. New friendships will be made, and these should derive from being with a more spiritually oriented crowd.

Something deep and mysterious may happen to you in December because, after the 26th, Mars slips into your mystical twelfth zone. If you haven't yet had an interest in spirituality and meditation, or a curiosity for why you are here, these Martian energies may be quite different from what you've previously experienced. You will feel a strong urge to delve into your true nature, and not rely on second-hand knowledge to reveal the truth to you.

2012
MONTHLY & DAILY PREDICTIONS

LIFE SHOULD BE MEASURED BY
HOW MANY MOMENTS TAKE YOUR
BREATH AWAY, INSTEAD OF HOW
MANY BREATHS YOU TAKE.

Anonymous

◎ JANUARY ◎

Monthly Highlight

You're a visionary right now, with Neptune hovering near your Sun sign. In the coming month, you must be careful not to let money rattle you. You are emotional but also spontaneous in the way you earn cash, and may be prone to spending without any real consideration for the consequences. These issues will be problematic for you, especially after the 13th.

1 You have a desire to work hard just now, and possibly to use the benefits of your profession either to change your residence or alter the circumstances in which you live.

2 You're invited to enter into an emotional relationship, but will you accept? You're inspired by someone, and this brings out some of your own creative and innovative ideas.

3 You are romantically inspired lately, but you may need to transform yourself to take full advantage of the situation. This might seem a little bit like too much hard work at the moment.

4 Rethink your personality and the effect you have on others. This is a time of new beginnings for yourself.

5 It's a social sort of day, and you have the opportunity to entertain at home. Making new friends, or at least mending relationships with old ones, will help set your personal affairs in order.

6 The social vibrations around you continue, and some sudden or abrupt opportunity will lift your day.

7 Today, there are problems on the home front, or you may feel betrayed by someone. Keep your wits about you.

8 If you're planning some travel at the moment, look more closely at the details. Missing a trivial piece of information could create a bigger problem than you would imagine.

9 Paperwork may overwhelm you just now, so you need to put a system in place that will allow you to deal with things in an orderly fashion. Sloppiness is not advised.

10 You are in an enterprising mood at the moment, but don't be too serious about work. You can do a good job and have fun at the same time, you know.

11 There could be a reunion of sorts today, and this might put you in touch with your past. Any misunderstandings or tension that you have been feeling can now be resolved.

12 You are quick to make a judgement today, possibly too quick, and may regret your haste. Fortunately, a friend will intervene and help you see the error of your ways before it is too late.

13 Loaning money is always fraught with danger, and now it may be time to collect. This could cause some strain on a relationship.

14 Trust your intuition in respect to a friend. Today, your social affairs are bright, but you may have an uneasy feeling about someone—this will prove to be correct.

15 If family or friends are experiencing emotional difficulties, you may need to mediate to help resolve the issue. Something good will come out of this.

16 Your health is focused just now, so take care to eat well and regulate your weight. Eating healthily requires a complete change of heart.

17 You may be concerned you don't have enough money to do what you want, but you know that just isn't true. Stop worrying about the future, and spend a little on a few treats to make yourself feel better.

18 Recently, you have had sleepless nights, concerning yourself with someone or some situation. You need self-discipline in both the day and the night to get some shuteye. Try some deep breathing.

19 You are confused, and this could cause a conflict with someone you love. Confronting situations are likely to arise, and you need to be calm and collected in the way you respond.

20 You may be presented with an offer of friendship—or perhaps someone has a deeper interest in you—which is not to your liking. You'll probably walk away.

21 There may be some correspondence issues concerning you at the moment, or a letter that has been delayed. Be patient and not too alarmed if you've missed the boat this time. Focus on something else for a while.

22 This is a period when many things will change, when you'll decide to renovate your circumstances. This includes making radical alterations to your financial systems.

23 Your disappointment just now may be rooted in your overactive imagination. However, it may also be that someone has been a little callous in their comments, which could cause you to be a bit sad.

24 You have the opportunity to communicate something of importance to the one you love today. On the other hand, there may be a friend whose time is up, and you realise you need to move on. Let go of relationships that are no longer serving you.

25 Someone new may enter your life right now, and this is fortuitous. You'll know who it is by the excellent communication and rapport you have with them.

26 You may want to take action immediately, but should first spend some time considering the consequences of your actions. By the same token, you mustn't be inconsistent or indecisive at this time.

27 Fortune is in the air today, but you need to deliberate very carefully before making a commitment and signing on the dotted line.

28 You may have friends or visitors drop in on you today. This is an opportunity for relaxation, and to mull over the past with some like minds.

29 Someone can release you from your tensions by offering you some help. You will be surprised that this person is not necessarily one of your closest friends, and will enjoy the kind gesture.

30 You will receive some good advice today. Have no doubts that if you act upon this now, you will reach a solution. But you may need to do a review of yourself to glean some deeper information about life as well.

31 Don't waste any money today. Although you are lucky, remember that it's what you save, not what you earn, which counts in the end.

◎ FEBRUARY ◎

Monthly Highlight

Your attractiveness and passion are at their peak at present, but be careful that Venus and Mars don't cause you to act irrationally in your relationships. Meeting new people is high on your agenda this month, but you're likely to make errors in the way you select friends. Listen to good advice.

You have some excellent opportunities for journeys around the 1st, and between the 8th and the 14th.

1 Sudden and unpredictable changes in romance could leave you dazed and confused. Be open to these changes, however, because when one door closes, another opens.

2 If you had problems with a friend, you may now realise that you were too quick to dismiss them. It's time to invite them back and make amends.

3 You will gain the respect and admiration of others through your clear and concise communication just now. Making the right decision is the focus of your life.

4 You may feel as if you're not receiving the attention and love that you should. The answer is to be more self-reliant, and to bolster your confidence from within. This transit will pass very quickly.

5 You'll hear some great news from afar, or from a person you've not seen for a while. You can gain insight, help and even financial assistance from an employer just now.

6 You should promote yourself actively, and not be afraid to show off your talents. You'll be recognised by the right people at this time.

7 Don't try to push your agenda too heavily today, because it could backfire. Others have the upper hand at this point, so take your time and let life resolve your issues for you.

8 You may find yourself away from home for a while, possibly due to business. Having to work longer hours than you prefer can be irritating, but the financial benefits are quite positive.

9 Pay strict attention to your personal attire today, and the way that you present yourself. You could find yourself suddenly in the limelight and needing to make a great impression.

10 You will require new information on your work or your industry during this period. Take the initiative to ferret out documents and facts that are going to improve your skills.

11 Put some energy into your relationships now if you want them to work. If you're not receiving a great deal of love, this may have to do with the extent of your own output.

12 You could be feeling insecure today, but this has more to do with being overly tired or pushing yourself beyond your limits. Don't forget to remind yourself that you're the one in control.

13 Lately, you have developed an interest in philosophical or metaphysical subjects, and now want to share this with someone. Some self-discoveries are imminent during this cycle.

14 Don't wait too long for that special call, because it may never arrive. You could be projecting your imagination onto a relationship that may not be destined to happen.

15 You should expand your discussions to include family members if you've made any plans recently. If you act without first consulting them, you could find yourself in hot water.

16 Be careful of new business ventures and of loaning money to others just now. There's a real danger you're being impulsive, and haven't looked at all the parts of the picture.

17 There might be some prosperous events occurring just now, with the Moon entering your zone of profits. Friends are instrumental in helping you achieve better results.

18 You feel great to have detached yourself from your problems, and can see the way forward by having a clearer mental picture of the situation. By honing your focus, you will find that past problems won't influence you as much anymore.

19 Someone you love may move away just now, and this will prompt you to increase your self-sufficiency. The departure could be due to an engagement or a marriage.

20 You may receive a gift today. Remember that you are rewarded not just financially, but by other people's gratitude, including their love and support for you.

21 You want news or something else work-related to improve, but could be feeling hamstrung at the moment. Do you call, or wait? Patience, I think, is the better virtue.

22 You could be feeling an undercurrent of mistrust between you and someone else. Don't make hasty judgements just yet, but observe their behaviour for a little longer.

23 You may lose an incentive in your work, which could punch a hole in your enthusiasm. Look at the bigger picture, for this will help counterbalance your disappointment.

24 You may be finishing up a project or partnership that wasn't quite all it was cut out to be. This could now require you to look for alternative sources of income.

25 Stop worrying about things over which you have no control. At present, there may be changes in your workplace, but unless you can do something about them, focus on something else.

26 You may be trying too hard, and relying too much on your own actions to achieve results. Let providence do a little bit of the work for you just now. Surrender.

27 You may have a lot of work on your plate, but with some determination you can get through this tough period, and feel revitalised as a result.

28 You may have to push harder to get your way just now, but this is the only course you have left to regain the respect you've lost.

29 You can fully realise your efforts this year, but periodically, there may be minor obstructions. Don't be thrown off-course by temporary obstacles.

☉ MARCH ☉

 Monthly Highlight

This month is powerful as the Sun transits your Sun sign. Get out and show others what you're capable of. Don't let family issues bog you down—there could potentially be moments of emotional blackmail from someone within the family. Between the 1st and the 15th, you need to focus on yourself, and balance your needs with those of others.

1   Dealing with powerful men, wealthy individuals and those in the upper echelons of society could rattle you today. Maintain your dignity, and don't feel inferior to anyone.

2   Your desires may be such that you feel you're incapable of achieving them. Stop comparing yourself to others, and watch the miracle of life taking place before your eyes.

3   Financial transactions, especially contracts, can prosper just now, because you are meticulous in every detail. Build things that are going to last.

4   If you're separated from someone you love at the moment, you need to accept that this is life's way of teaching you some lessons. Don't have any regrets.

5   Unexpected good news in your workplace gives you cause for celebration! A change of pace is a welcome relief.

6   If you're feeling vulnerable, you may find it difficult to control those who have the upper hand. Just go about your business without paying too much attention to them.

7   You are too compulsive about your work and business activities during this cycle, so you need to get away, relax and unwind for a while. Stop making life harder for yourself.

8   If you decide to take a short trip, be careful who you choose to go with you. This could make or break your holiday.

9   You may have to postpone some of the tasks allocated to you, because you find them a little too complicated. Don't forget to enlist the help of others in these matters.

10 You could have a run in with a powerbroker or someone who uses manipulative techniques to get their way just now. You have to be one step ahead of them.

11 Your passions are particularly strong, but you may be confused as to whether or not you're putting your energies into the right person. There's no rush to discover the answer.

12 Someone may let you down right now, and just when you need them the most. You may be momentarily devastated by this event, but you'll quickly recover.

13 Accept an offer to develop your talents because eventually you will have a great opportunity to put them to good use, and even earn money from them.

14 Focusing on your communications just now could yield both professional and personal surprises. This is an excellent time to get positive feedback.

15 If a relative has some problems at the moment, you may need to help them. These could be centred on a legal issue.

16 Your health is good, so don't become a hypochondriac and believe that there's something going on that simply isn't. If you're unconvinced, get a checkup and put your mind at ease.

17 You're expecting a payment, tax cheque or other small windfall, but it could be delayed. I suggest you don't spend that money before you get it!

18 The future is only what you make of it in the present. Try managing your time better and improving your situation. Share your ideas.

19 You are bound to someone who makes you miserable, but you've become addicted to the experience. Break the chains that bind you.

20 If you choose to purchase a gift for a friend or relative, make sure you're not focusing too much on the cost, rather than on the experience of generosity and gratitude.

21 Some vital information arrives just now. It could help you break free of a circumstance that has held you back. A short journey may be necessary to fill in any gaps.

22 You're anxious about money because you feel that someone else is calling the shots. It is time to assert yourself more than you have in the past.

23 You're probably giving more in a relationship than you're receiving. Balance this by talking about your feelings. Watch out for vehicle mishaps and the service aspect associated with them today.

24 You are pretending to be happy in a situation, but your internal conflict and emotional upheaval tells a very different story. The inner must agree with the outer if you are to be fully satisfied in life.

25 If you're finding it hard to make a choice just now, a friend will come to your assistance. You will realise there is an alternative to the circumstances in which you are living.

26 You need to put yourself first today, and forget about other people's problems, even if they seem pressing. Your key word just now is self-attention.

27 Someone may share some ideas with you today and although they are unrelated to what you are doing, they could trigger a whole new series of thoughts. You can look forward to a brighter tomorrow.

28 Although people want your company, you are feeling like a hermit and don't want to socialise just now. You are under no compulsion, however.

29 You may be the recipient of extra money or cash bonuses that turn up. Remember, this kind of event is the perfect reflection of the efforts you are making in your work. You deserve what you receive.

30 You could attract a favour at the moment, which will put you at a distinct advantage. An older woman may be instrumental in the outcome.

31 You may have to do battle to make your point today. After all is said and done, however, you should shake hands and make up.

⊚ APRIL ⊚

 Monthly Highlight

Mars is retrograde, so issues surrounding relationships will be tough this month especially if someone is doing back-flips on you after you plan a course of action. The 3rd until the 5th will be an uncertain period, one in which you will be second-guessing yourself.

Debts will reach an unmanageable level if you aren't careful this month. You may need to take some drastic measures after the 24th.

---

1 Your cup is spilling over and you're not even aware of it. It's time to look at what you have, rather than at what you don't. You've overlooked the generosity of a friend recently.

---

2 You want things cleared up at work, but you need to handle your job a little better as well. This includes dealing with the politics of a particular situation.

---

3 Social occasions are plentiful just now, but there may be additional expenses to keep up with the crowd.

4 You are looking in the wrong places for happiness and material security at the moment. What you seek is, more than likely, within the four walls of your own home.

5 You'll be caught off guard by a surprise, a confrontation, or a petty remark today. However, you mustn't react to it, otherwise you will only escalate the problem.

6 The Moon and Venus are in an excellent placement to bring you happiness just now, and even chance encounters. This may lead to increased networking and possibly also money.

7 Don't let temporary dissatisfaction cause you to make rash decisions about moving. Stick with it for a little while longer.

8 You'll make a discovery about a place or cultural environment that you want to investigate. This could start the ball rolling for some long journeys.

9 You may have tried or tested a new method to improve your workflow, only to find that the old way is better. Restore things to their previous setup.

10 Work is on your mind, and you have loads of energy for achieving your goals just now. Venus and Uranus indicate opportunities to earn money through domestic activities or property.

11 You may find a relationship is developing more quickly than you can cope with. It's up to you to apply the brakes.

12 Your emotions will be nostalgic as you glance over your shoulder at the past. However, don't be afraid to move into new or unknown territory on your path of life.

13 You could be reticent about attending a fancy dress party or an event at which you might feel awkward. Even if you are overly self-conscious, you will, more than likely, enjoy yourself.

14 Succinct correspondence with someone is necessary just now, so that you can either formalise or keep a record of what has been said.

15 A family member may go away for a while. You mustn't be sad about this because everyone needs a break at some point.

16 Tempering your lifestyle and, in particular, your eating and drinking habits is essential today. Whatever physical discomfort you experience is your own doing.

17 You have to start juggling finances better, because you can no longer blame an economic downturn for the state of them. Look more closely at yourself.

18 You have several projects on the go, but may find it hard prioritising them. That's the task at hand.

19 You know things are not going to continue along the same path, but through fear of change you may try to avoid the inevitable. You have to be ruthless.

20 You are emotionally rewarded by what you see in your loved ones. An admirer may also give you a greater sense of self-worth today.

21 Being just and fair is sometimes difficult. You may be placed in a position where you need to choose one person over another.

22 You may be getting involved with the wrong person and unable to see the complicated nature of their personality. Study others more closely.

23 You'll be in for disappointment if you believe that everything is going to look after itself without you taking any responsibility. Have a Plan B ready.

24 It may be time to break the ties with someone who has been emotionally disappointing you. This has to do with reclaiming your own power.

25 Take the time to act on a new resolution and eliminate bad habits. You'll feel even more empowered through this.

26 You're particularly concerned about having to act as judge, jury and even executioner today. It's best to let others come forward for this task.

27 You can act as a bridge over troubled water for a friend just now. Don't be afraid to allocate time for friends in need.

28 Visitors may prove to be an annoyance, especially if you feel obliged to invite them over. A simple no for the moment won't ruin the friendship.

29 Your stars are lucky at present, and your willpower is on the increase, both of which can help developments in areas of your life that were previously obstructed.

30 You will need guidance if things seem to be falling apart just now. It's likely you aren't seeing the whole picture, so why not try stepping back from the situation for a while?

◎ MAY ◎

Monthly Highlight

Saturn performs some transformative actions on your deep, inner self and psyche this month. Confronting issues from your past between the 5th and the 13th may be unpleasant, but it will end up refreshing your mind and soul.

A trip in the latter part of the month, perhaps after the 26th, will be an excellent reprieve from some of the pressures of life.

1 You have the strength to implement your resolutions just now. This is a great start to the month.

2 The Moon in your seventh house indicates that you'll be a star with your partner during this month. You'll find deeper meaning in your relationship.

3 Offering to help someone financially will come back to you because your karma is powerful.

4   You must resolve the issue of a past romance if it still affects you, even only periodically. Perhaps you need to call the person in question, to tie up loose ends?

5   You will be met with disapproval regarding a plan you wish to carry out. A family member is being unreasonable just now.

6   You have to try alternative approaches to resolve a recurring situation. Your previous attempts may have failed, but you'll be encouraged by the response just now.

7   There are conflicts on the home front. Do everything you can to avoid an argument. Keep peace for the sake of unity.

8   You may agree to go on an outing or journey knowing full well you can't afford it. Cast aside your pride, and be honest about the situation.

9   Go back over documents and other contractual paperwork to make sure you haven't missed anything. This will be tedious, but very freeing once complete.

10   A business proposal might not necessarily be in your best interests. You need adequate exit clauses, as well as mutual lurks and perks.

11 The Moon in Jupiter favours friendship, but also the realisation of where you may have been falling down in the partnership. Rectification is your key word today.

12 If you and a friend are overly emotional about something, you may find that a third party, a mutual friend, is helpful in resolving the problem.

13 Simple pleasures are the order of the day. You don't have to embellish or go overboard. This could include enjoying your own company.

14 You are curious about the world just now, and want more interaction with others, perhaps even through social networks on the Internet.

15 Just when you thought you were going to have a hard day, someone—a friend or relative—will call with good news.

16 Venus moves retrograde, therefore you have concerns about matters on the home front. Health issues may need your attention, particularly of a dental nature.

17 You have a bright idea today, and need to follow it up. It may not be the invention of the century, just a clever, quirky little notion that will bring more pleasure to you and someone else.

18 A powerful woman of an intellectual calibre may sway your opinions today, but it's probably for the better.

19 Today, friendships, lively talk and common interests will encourage your future partnerships.

20 A token of goodwill will be appreciated just now. But be careful: this may be a small form of bribery in disguise.

21 You've been kept in the dark over a certain matter, and will probably feel foolish when you see the issue come to light. Use this as a learning experience.

22 You may say something inadvertently around this time only to later realise the error of your ways. Sort things out as soon as you are aware of them.

23 The Moon in your fifth house of creativity means finding the courage to explore one of your hidden talents. But you may have to sacrifice another equally satisfying activity to do this.

24 A huge problem you've had at home—or an otherwise big concern—comes to an end. You can now relax and enjoy yourself.

25 You find yourself attracting some attention today, perhaps unintentionally. You'll have to adjust yourself to deal with it.

26 It's time for action. You may need to rule with an iron fist if you're going to get things done and command the reciprocal respect you desire.

27 You are battle-weary, and wondering whether you should continue in the same role. It's a time for reflection.

28 You realise you must now complete those last-minute modifications to your house, especially if you have visitors coming. You'll feel embarrassed if your home doesn't look as good as it could.

29 You'll be aware of a higher presence in your life, but communicating this to someone could prove awkward. Keep your realisations to yourself just now.

30 Knowledge is the gateway to greater earnings and a fine reputation. You may consider extending your field of knowledge through a course or degree during this period.

31 You may be the witness of a theft or petty crime and will not know what to do. Let your conscience guide you.

⊚ JUNE ⊚

Monthly Highlight

You could be feeling down, perhaps because you think others have more than you. In the first week of the month, resist the temptation to keep up with the Joneses.

Work hard, especially from the 4th till the 10th. You can make great headway in your career. A lucky break in contracts and other business communications will occur between the 20th and the 24th.

1   Securing an improved lifestyle sometimes involves particularly big sacrifices. You may find it hard to make the break.

2   You have the desire to succeed at this point in time, and your creative imagination may make you obsessive. Try to keep everything practical.

3   You are feeling run down or angry with yourself for some reason. Set the standards high, by all means, but achieve the results step by step.

4   There are opportunities to meet new people today, or at least be enamoured by someone of striking appearance. These may occur through business or a work-related activity.

5   You are feeling vital and alive just now. Could this be because the lunar eclipse is releasing some of your deep-seated energies?

6   You are carrying a heavy load at the moment. There's no shame in changing plans to adjust to the situation.

7   Something in your established routine may be subject to a dramatic change just now, and it could be out of your control.

8   You need to lay low today, but still have some obligations to perform. This could make you irritated.

9   You've forgotten to do something, and may realise it only when it's too late. Once the opening to a path closes, you might just have to accept your fate.

10   You could be privy to a new business or financial idea around this time. It may look good on paper, but you know in your heart that it simply will not work.

11 This is a good day to sit down with others and have an in-depth pow-wow. People will be receptive to your presentation.

12 Don't be too impressionable when you meet someone today. Putting others on a pedestal sets you up for a fall.

13 You may win an argument, only to find that several other people have a low estimation of you as a consequence. Be prudent with your words just now.

14 Your brain is fully activated today, but, as a result, you may create indecision for yourself about a certain matter. Leave it for a day or two.

15 You're imagining that things are worse than they are. This could be because too many people are complaining about their own difficulties. Rise above them.

16 You are picking up the slack while others loaf off. Put your foot down, and demand that everyone contribute equally.

17 A decision has been made regarding your work or finances, and now there's no turning back. Enjoy the ride!

18 You're not comfortable with a particular aspect of your relationship, and this could create tensions in your home for a while.

19 Believe it or not, a friend—although possibly not a close one—will be a mentor for you now. Listen carefully to their words of wisdom.

20 You are frenetic today, and need at least two or three more pairs of hands to help you. Swallow your pride and ask for assistance.

21 If you've been foolhardy and spent too much money (or worse still, gambled it away), then you've got no one else to blame for your difficult financial circumstances.

22 You are presented with numerous choices at present, so your intuition needs to be as sharp as possible. Rely on your heart, not your head.

23 You may have had high expectations of a project, only to find out now that the outcome was less than you expected. Cut your losses if necessary.

24 Being overly preoccupied with money may cause your partner to withdraw for a while. Balance money and love.

25 Spending time alone is different to being lonely. Know the difference today, and your inner light of understanding may begin to shine.

26 You mustn't force a decision right now, and if you remain calm, your patience will reward you with an inner, still voice telling you the correct path of action.

27 You are becoming more and more self-reliant, but there are still times when you need help. Don't be scared to pick up the phone and call someone.

28 By balancing your financial and emotional issues, you will allow for a transformation to occur naturally. This is a powerful and spiritual day.

29 You may be anxious to learn the truth from someone about a situation in which you were both involved. When you hear the facts, you'll be relieved.

30 You may need to flex your muscles and posture a little to get your way in work today. It is, however, possible do this without displaying too much ego.

☉ JULY ☉

Monthly Highlight

You are happy due to the positioning of Venus and Jupiter, but try not to be gushy. Being overly sentimental may ruin the opportunity for a new relationship. Use some intellect to win over others. Excellent social opportunities—arising from the 2nd to the 5th, and then again from the 17th till the 23rd—ensure that July is a happy and fulfilling month.

1 You will fall prey to apathy if you are not careful today. However, if someone pushes you into action, you may retaliate, and this could create an argument.

2 Please do not take someone for granted just now. Watch for the hidden signals in their body language and non-verbal communication. They need your attention.

3   Trade, finance and negotiations could be part of your schedule today. However, you may have to struggle on your own if you are truly serious about going for your dreams.

4   Wait to see what your partner or lover wants do before making your own decision today. As a result, you may spontaneously choose to leave or go out somewhere.

5   Someone may declare their love or affection for you. Although you are not completely surprised by this, you will be flattered.

6   You want to withdraw from a friendship just now, to give the other person an opportunity to look over their actions and see what they have done wrong.

7   You want to splurge today, and do something for yourself. Call a friend and go shopping! Once you start to reward yourself, you'll see that this, in turn, gives positive messages to the universe.

8   If you feel there is no give and take in your relationships at the moment, you should not dismiss this lightly. Assert your worthiness in all your current partnerships.

9   If you don't act on your dreams when you have the chance, you may just miss them. Today's the day for planning and aiming high. Don't let people's negative attitudes distract you from your goals.

10   Your imagination may be too strong just now, and not in keeping with the reality of your financial situation. The planets seem to be saying work hard, but also, work smart.

11   You have hopes of resuscitating a relationship, but could be a little too optimistic about the truth of the situation. Sometimes you need to accept things as they are and move on.

12   The emphasis today is on study, but also on travelling to gain more information. Social activities tie in nicely with educational pursuits.

13   Your good fortune is running high just now, and you could finance a premeditated risk or even just a wee punt.

14   You are not as weak as you think you are. It's your thinking that is weak, not you. Change your attitude, and assert yourself in your current course of action.

15 The planetary energies do not favour a career shift or job interview just now. Work harder on your interview skills and communication techniques before taking this kind of step.

16 A potential triumph in speculation is indicated. Investigate what stocks or investments are likely to give returns, even just modest ones.

17 There's no doubt that you have the vital drive and enterprise to work out some of your troubles today, but at the same time, tension and pressure will make a difficult labour of the entire process.

18 Family members could inconvenience you today, as well as upset you by saying something behind your back. Issues of trust may weigh heavily on your mind.

19 Although you think there is no way to bridge a difference of opinion, rest assured that you will, in time, make friends again with someone who has deserted you.

20 You need to shed your skin, so to speak, to let the real you shine forth. You have the ability to make an impression on someone that counts today.

21 You may go to extraordinary lengths to accomplish your goals at the moment, but don't forget to consider whether or not the results are worth the effort.

22 You could become rather fixated on whatever you are doing just now, and this, in turn, will cause a great deal of anxiety. You are trying too hard to please someone, and not getting benefits from those efforts.

23 Pushing yourself past your limits might be a distinct warning that you are not operating with the right motives, and may be undermining your physical health.

24 You can widen the scope of your everyday activities right now, and increase your circle of influence. Locking yourself behind closed doors is no way to experience life or to enhance yourself.

25 You need a trusted operator to help you with some of the problems you are experiencing. For example, financial matters sometimes need an expert to wade through the complex laws surrounding them.

26 Some confusion over the feelings of another person and their attitude towards you will soon clear up, so don't lose sleep over the situation.

27 You may be pushing your luck a little too much today, even if what you're recommending to people makes sense. Let them live their lives to their own level of experience.

28 Something unusual could occur with a call by a friend. You may be surprised at what you learn, but may find it frustrating not being able to divulge this knowledge to anyone else.

29 Play it safe today, and don't take any chances by pushing others on controversial topics. They could strongly disagree, especially if the discussion drifts into religious or political terrain.

30 You can be decorative without being outlandish, and just now, that creative spark within you may be aching to express itself perhaps in some form of interior design or art. This kind of thing does cost money, however.

31 Unfortunately, some of your tastes are a little unconventional at present, and friends may disagree with your approach to things. However, you should stand up for your beliefs, irrespective of general opinion.

☙ AUGUST ☙

 Monthly Highlight

You'll be down this month if you focus on things that are unimportant. Don't sweat the small stuff, as they say. The 1st and the 2nd may require you to step out of the picture for a while, and regain your energy and confidence.

Things look better for you after the 8th, when a surprise on the home front lifts your spirits. The 14th to the 16th is great for intimate encounters, but the 17th and the 18th could prove frustrating with a friend.

---

1 'He who laughs best, laughs last' is a saying you should commit to memory and use as the day progresses. Don't get too caught up in others' passing statements. You're getting too personal.

---

2 Now is the time to promote yourself, to get out there and show others just what you're made of. This will assist in your negotiations as well.

---

3 For some reason, you're getting tongue-tied today, and your speech isn't flowing as well as it usually does. Find the underlying causes.

4 You may be creating work simply to distract yourself from a personal problem. However, you must address it, because no amount of avoidance is going to solve it.

5 Today, you need a steady tongue and a focused mind if you are to avoid feeling highly strung, and not get yourself into trouble.

6 If you want people to understand you, you have to be clear and consistent in your speech. You are sending mixed signals today.

7 An admirer may want to spend some time with you. This could involve taking a trip or short journey.

8 Don't get caught up in the rush for fame, power and glory. Keep your feet planted firmly on the ground, and never forget your roots.

9 You may uncover something of value today, or find a lost item. This is also a good day to purchase a lottery ticket.

10 If you handle your work with skill and diligence, you'll be able to complete all your tasks on time. Strangely, though, love will be more important than work in this period.

11 Business matters are associated with your partner or loved one today, and discussions about your home—along with rental or sale issues—will be the focus.

12 You mustn't let a minor frustration with a close friend cause you too much tension. You could get flustered, but remember that what you do in this situation is your own choice.

13 You may have to change your mind on something just now, and although that could cause you some embarrassment, you know it's the right thing to do.

14 You could be challenged or blocked by someone via e-mail. It's best to sleep on the problem before doing anything rash.

15 There could be someone in your family who is suffering physically or is constrained by illness. This is a day when your compassion will rise to the occasion.

16 You may be run down and needing the help of someone else after extending yourself to others for too long.

17 You might be lucky in work just now, but could feel a little disappointed that a postponement or delay will not give you the results as quickly as you want them. Don't worry: the money is forthcoming.

18 Are you doing too much at the moment? Even though you have the drive and energy to take on many projects, you may be too distracted to finish any one completely.

19 You might be worried that you don't have the level of support from your friends that you would like. However, you are probably unaware of just how many supporters you do have. Think carefully.

20 It's not a good idea to borrow books or personal items at the moment, because you may misplace them, then end up out of pocket having to pay for the lost goods.

21 The number 8 is lucky for you just now, and if you are planning to buy a ticket or gamble on something, this could be a positive omen.

22 You could be frustrated by someone's cagey behaviour today. Trying to bed down the relationship—or at least gauge where they stand with you—is not going to be easy.

23 Your unfulfilled desires could be playing on your mind at present. It's best to enjoy the moment and cherish what you have, rather than bemoan what you don't.

24 You have spiritual energies affecting you lately that will impact positively on your working life. Doing the right thing seems to be the key phrase for you at present.

25 You may be suspicious of someone who wishes to form a partnership with you on a project, but be assured that their intentions are noble.

26 You are juggling too many social engagements today. It's entirely up to you, however, as to which of these you choose, and how much energy you put into them.

27 Although a long-held goal seems to be in sight—at last!—you mustn't declare yourself successful just yet. Another minor hiccup may need to be dealt with first.

28 Today, a new avenue may present itself, after a discussion with someone. Finances look good.

29 You have lost some paperwork that is, perhaps, essential for a tax return or for cashing in on some purchase points. Sift through your stuff again, and look a little harder.

30 It's only a matter of time before you get what you want, so don't be too hard on yourself. Your mind is clear in its pursuit, so trust your logic.

31 You can reach a positive conclusion just now, but if there are too many cooks spoiling the broth, as the saying goes, you'll never get anywhere. Take the lead.

❂ SEPTEMBER ❂

Monthly Highlight

You're keen to materialise your dreams, and the combined influence of Venus and Neptune gives you excellent insight and intuitive clues as to what to do. You can take a punt between the 8th and the 12th, but be careful around the 13th and the 14th, because your health may not be up to par.

You will have some fun times in your one-on-one relationships in September, especially if you're married. The period from the 15th to the 19th should prove fruitful.

Don't let antagonism undermine your decision-making processes in the latter part of the month. Keep calm.

1 You're trying to play the martyr just now, by proving you can do so many things. However, your endeavours will be harmed by your tiredness and lack of mental focus. Decline what you can't do.

2 You need some spiritual support or a foundation for your actions right now. Some financial assistance wouldn't hurt, either. Don't be afraid to ask for help.

3 A friend is going to pay you back for an outstanding debt, but your emotional attachment could cool off in the meantime. Sometimes you have no control over how relationships end.

4 Take care in the way you dish out discipline or punishment today, particularly with someone who may simply be the messenger.

5 You may start to feel quite tired with individuals who aren't pulling their weight. Will you say something, or let it slide?

6 A deal or promised opportunity may be all talk and no action. You are not scrutinising the offer or the person who's making promises carefully enough.

7 You mustn't begrudge the fact that you have to spend a little bit of money on entertainment just now. Enjoy the company of good friends, and let your generosity take flight.

8   You may have trouble with an older man who is used to ruling the roost. Although you may want to travel, you may not have the means to do so.

9   The good news you are expecting to hear has some conditions attached. You may find that these all but mar the original prospect.

10 You're in the company of children or those much younger in age today. This will inspire you and give you more enthusiasm for life.

11 The Moon and Mercury together highlight love affairs and marriage just now. However, there is a tug-of-war between your sense of commitment and your freedom.

12 You may be excited about getting a new toy. This may simply be a way of nourishing yourself if you haven't got someone to do it for you. Computers and gadgets are featured just now.

13 You feel as if you're making a difference in the lives of others, and could therefore be recommended to someone who will bring you some emotional fulfilment in return.

14 Although you may have the opportunity to go out, your budget may not allow for the expense. There's no harm in postponing your plan until a better day.

15 You might make tentative plans to get together with a good friend, which is a good idea because they may not be available for a while after this.

16 If you're feeling a shortness of breath, palpitations or anxiety attacks, this may have to do with the pressure you're experiencing at work. Talk to your employer about staggering the workload.

17 You have the money to make things happen, but not the agreement from those who control the way you do things. Negotiation is necessary.

18 What seemed like an impossible task may be made a lot easier by some new information you receive today. A friend is willing to help.

19 Although you may be angry with a friend who has let you down, please give consideration to the circumstances or context in which this happened. Forces outside their control may have had something to do with it.

20 You will receive a favour from someone, but may feel obliged to reciprocate. The positive feelings from their generosity may be overshadowed as a result.

21 You are interested in making enquiries about cultural or social activities that will benefit your work. For example, organising import-export opportunities may be on the agenda.

22 Your efforts to complete your work and meet your deadlines may be thwarted by someone who is trying to dominate you. You need to be creative in getting around them.

23 You may feel like a friend or a group of friends is against you just now, as if something subversive is going on. Have faith in the power of nature to resolve this.

24 Although you feel connected to someone, you may need to call a spade a spade to correct them on their behaviour today. Initially, they may fight you, but will eventually see the logic in your statements.

25 You can begin a new course of self-study or meditation just now, and make great strides in becoming self-actualised. A retreat may be of interest to you.

26 Stop trying to live up to others' expectations of what you should be. It doesn't matter what anyone else thinks—it's up to you.

27 You could inherit a half-baked idea that can be worked into something practical and valuable. Recycling seems to be a key word today.

28 You may feel intimidated by a powerful person, but they are actually quite insecure on the inside. See them for who and what they are.

29 You can resolve arguments at home and put to bed a longstanding disagreement today. At work, someone may disagree with one of your choices.

30 You must trust yourself just now, and if your gut feelings tell you to go with something, you should. Do not compare your relationship to others', however.

☉ OCTOBER ☉

Monthly Highlight

You have an urge to travel, but should do that in the first week of the month because business and professional responsibilities may get the better of you later on.

Look carefully at expenses, and whether or not you are capable of helping someone through their present difficult patch. Caution should be exercised between the 15th and the 20th.

1 Now is the time to make some environmental changes, but also to look at new ways of handling money. There could be a shift in what you value just now.

2 You should look at money in different ways. Straight cash is not always the best form of payment. Investigate forms of 'elegant' currency.

3 You must continue on the path you have chosen, even if it is a little difficult. Persistence is your key word, and this will pay off.

4   If you've been hanging on to the past, now is the time to free yourself and move forward. A negative feeling that has been revolving in your mind will start to fade away.

5   Just as the desire to do something arises, you will be surprised to find life providing you with a hint—or even a clear direction—of how to go about it. Trust your instincts.

6   You have mixed emotions as to whether to befriend someone today or not. There could be disapproval from third parties.

7   The discussion of a transfer to another office or location for work, even temporarily, may cause problems on the home front. Extensive consultation will be necessary before a decision is made.

8   Issues of travel arise now, but something will be missing, or there will be disagreement over which destinations to go to.

9   You want to get involved with someone, but feel as if your space in the relationship is far too occupied by their personality. It's all a matter of give and take.

10 It's best to take some time out if, so far, you've had no luck in finding solutions for the project you're currently working on. The irony is that by taking a break, you'll get much more accomplished.

11 Are you facing the right direction? If the signpost says Melbourne is this way, and you wish to go to Brisbane, you're obviously on the wrong path. Stop and rethink your journey.

12 You could be moody just now, and with Saturn still influencing your deeper emotions and ethical decisions, you will need to be adaptable.

13 You might feel bad about a decision because it impacted adversely on someone else. However, would they have approached the situation any differently to you?

14 You must not put everything on the line simply for a win. There are further ramifications to consider at the moment.

15 An employer or co-worker may do you a favour today, but they will have ulterior motives. You don't trust them because of things you've heard on the grapevine.

16 You have the opportunity to take on additional work for extra money, but will the remuneration be worth the extra pressure?

17 Money owing to you could be slow in coming, and due to some technical or staffing difficulties, your pay will be late. Hopefully, you have a buffer for these sorts of situations.

18 Getting the ball rolling on a venture may involve much more than you had planned. There may be complaints on the home front if you don't fulfil your domestic duties.

19 Talking with a friend can be enlightening now, and their encouragement will help you with clarity. But you still have one missing factor: the courage to act on your desires.

20 Today, you may receive an invitation to go somewhere unusual. You can, but it's also best to bring along a trusted friend to monitor the situation.

21 You might hear some gossip through an e-mail or third-party letter that undermines your faith or confidence in a friend. You need to broach the topic gently with them.

22 Setting up for a function or organising a group of friends takes up more time than you originally allocated. Some time management and delegation will be necessary.

23 In your spontaneous desire to be generous, you may offer to pay the bill for lunch, only to discover the price is much higher than you had expected. This will teach you to think carefully in future!

24 'The world is your oyster' right now. It doesn't matter what you choose to do, it will all work out and bring you great satisfaction. Roll the dice and flow with it, Pisces.

25 You look up to someone who has gone through many of the same experiences that you, too, may soon have to face. Trust their words of advice, because they can help you short-circuit impending problems, especially in relationships.

26 You are projecting some of your own shortcomings onto someone else. Try to take responsibility for your feelings, even if you need to walk away and say no for a while.

27 You may be concerned about an inheritance, particularly if there is lingering competitiveness between you and a sibling. Try not to think about these things until a more appropriate time.

28 You will be warmly received by a group of strangers, much to your amazement. Has someone said something nice about you prior to this meeting? It doesn't matter. Great camaraderie can be expected today.

29 Take the middle ground if you are undecided about a course of action at the moment. You want the outcome to be win-win for all concerned.

30 You are overly emotional just now, and the event you believe is causing it is not the real source of your pain. Analyse yourself more deeply.

31 You may temporarily have to take responsibility for someone else's children or pets. However, before blindly rushing into the situation, think through the ramifications.

⊚ NOVEMBER ⊚

Monthly Highlight

This is an excellent time to communicate your needs to your employer, or to venture forth and start a new job. Between the 12th and the 16th, you'll be ferreting out information that can help your cause in a professional sense.

1 Someone is thinking of selecting you to help them in a project or initiative. Pay attention to details today. There may be no money in this to start with, but it could lead to bigger and brighter things.

2 Take the appropriate time to word your correspondence correctly at the moment. If you rush, it will later come back to haunt you.

3 A legal matter may need to be dealt with, or you may be called upon to mediate between warring factions just now.

4 It's time to sit back, relax and enjoy the fruits of your work. You feel like an emperor or empress today, and so you should—you deserve it.

5 You may be taken aback and put off guard by someone's statements today. If you have history with them, you need to be prepared for what they're going to throw at you.

6 It's just as important to understand the politics of a situation as it is to understand the work at hand. Someone can give you some insights in this area today.

7 You may need to make a payment on a ticket, or there will be additional travel expenses you hadn't bargained on. Remember that excess luggage is charged by the kilo.

8 You could meet someone in transit today, and have a thoroughly good conversation with them. You'll realise just how fast time flies when you're having fun.

9 You may need to help your partner with a complex contractual or communications issue just now. Advise them that the time is ripe for a change.

10   You could be upset or discouraged at just how much effort you've been making to save money lately, but still seem to be getting nowhere. Look after the pennies, and the dollars will look after themselves.

11   If you are in a relationship, today could be one of those days where you feel like leaving, or simply getting out and not having anything to do with your partner. Time out is sometimes a good idea.

12   You are irritable today, because you've committed yourself to a situation out of obligation. There's nothing much you can do but grin and bear it now.

13   You should never go guarantor for anyone lightly, even family. You may find yourself cornered by a request to sign on the dotted line. Think of an alternative strategy to satisfy all parties concerned.

14   The solar eclipse today is important, and indicates that you must not be rash or impulsive in leaving your current situation. Just let the issue percolate a little longer.

15 Communication continues with your family, but you may start to feel detached and disconnected from them. You may not necessarily be growing apart, but you are growing, and they may not be.

16 Be careful of your health just now, because you're blindly living life the same way you always have. It's time for you to make some important changes to improve yourself.

17 Someone you consider a friend is behaving badly, and you might have to say something about it. If you fear losing their friendship as a result, then you're missing the point.

18 You may be stabbed in the back just now: betrayed by a friend or even a lover. Trust your intuition on some of the signals you are receiving.

19 Spending money may be a blessing in disguise. As long as you invest in the right way (for example, in renovating your home), you will see a return on the money you spend.

20 You are treading water just now, and may not know which way to proceed. But you don't need to make a decision immediately! Sleep on it, and you'll be surprised at how quickly the solution will come to you.

21 You may be promised something by your boss, but circumstances obstruct them from making good on this. They may end up feeling bitter about it.

22 Remaining consistent in your attitude will be a challenge just now. Disciplining your mind is the most important thing.

23 You could feel explosive today, because things don't necessarily go your way. You are likely to say and do things you will later regret, even if you have just cause for doing so.

24 You finally understand that dwelling on the past is of no use because it doesn't serve you. Let go of it, and start over with a fresh slate.

25 You should direct your energies towards the material goals you want just now. Your concentration will be powerful, and mysteriously, the resources and people you need will come forward.

26 If you are having difficulties with someone who is lazy and unmotivated, pushing them is only going to cause a backlash. Teach by example, if you can.

27 Mercury moves direct today, and matters that were previously in limbo become much clearer. A delayed decision can now be made, and you have the green light to move forward.

28 You are content with family life today, and prefer to be a couch potato. Watching a movie, sipping a glass of red wine and kicking back is just what the doctor ordered.

29 You'll be glad to see two family members finally resolve their differences. This will bring peace and harmony to the household.

30 Stop throwing good money after bad with a renovation project at home. It's probably best to demolish it and start over again.

❂ DECEMBER ❂

 Monthly Highlight

Legal issues, ethics and spirituality dominate your mental and emotional landscape this month. Sorting through what's worthwhile and practical—or not, as the case may be—forms the larger part of your inner task. From the 7th until the 15th, spend some quiet time re-evaluating your life's mission.

From the 19th to the 22nd, opportunities to earn more money will be a welcome surprise.

---

1 It's time to call a truce, particularly with neighbours. If, lately, there's been some sort of tension between you and those around you, it's a day to reconcile.

---

2 You want to move forward with something—you don't want idle chit-chat and endless discussions. Whatever the project is, get on with it, even if others have a problem with how you're going about it.

---

3 It should be easy to realise that your progress in work is an organic process. Don't be scared to venture away from your original goals or plans for success.

4 You may have difficulties reconciling your philosophical beliefs with those of a new lover. This is most important, and if you can't find compromise, it's probably best to call it a day.

5 You'll be pleasantly surprised by your partner or lover when they offer to assist you in some area of your life. You may wonder what it is they want, but cast aside your suspicions for the moment.

6 If you're in a business partnership, you may be thinking of bringing in a third party or dumping your current partner. However, consider that there may be some truth to the saying 'better the devil you know than the devil you don't'.

7 You may want to go shopping and purchase some new furniture or artworks for your home. Don't skimp on costs, because it may end up being a good future investment.

8 You may be angry at the way one of your friends is treating her partner, but feel constrained in saying something. The best thing you can do is lead by example.

9   This is the time to consider whether cutting your losses is the best option. Proceeding further (and with more and more costs) on a dispute or legal matter may run you into the ground.

10   Your imagination—regarding your work and what's possible in it—may seem far fetched to others, and maybe even to yourself, but you should believe in your dreams.

11   If you are being mistreated, you must not continue to be a doormat. Stand up for yourself.

12   You may have embarked on a course of action based on the information provided, only to find that your managers have changed their minds. Rather than losing your cool, simply adjust yourself to their new directives.

13   You are prepared to try working in a different vein or using different technologies. This is a big step, but the time saved will be quite significant, indeed.

14   Your mind is expanding now, because you see so many different possibilities in the world around you. If you're in a relationship that's hindering those possibilities, you'll do something about it now.

15 You must not let too many people's emotions get in the road at a roundtable discussion at home. Stick to the facts, and under no circumstances bring up the past.

16 You could find it difficult getting the health care you need for a particular problem. You may need to travel far and wide to get expert advice.

17 You've made a decision about someone prematurely, without thoroughly understanding their personality. You'll now see the cracks starting to form in their character.

18 Your preoccupations with business, money and your social life are blinding you to the problem of someone close to you at home.

19 You're hearing gossip about yourself, but can't believe it's originating from the source that people say it is. Confront the alleged culprit.

20 An unexpected career opportunity is awaiting you, but you mustn't procrastinate. Return the call immediately.

21 Important news regarding work prospects will excite you, but do you have everything in order, such as your curriculum vitae? Get to it.

22 You are frustrated by ineffectual pen pushers who don't seem to be doing anything to solve your problem. Go above someone's head to get the job done.

23 Empty promises need to be sidestepped just now. If you're relying on someone to do something for you, in the end, you may be better off doing it yourself.

24 With Christmas now on your doorstep, it is a good time to regain some of your strength to get through the next week or two. Improved conditions in your finances will reduce your worries.

25 It's Christmas, and you may be too busy looking after others to worry about yourself. Try to find some balance in this respect.

26 You may finally realise that your true family is not determined by blood, so much as by spirit. Extending your circle of 'family' will be important now.

27 Older and more experienced friends appeal to you just now, and can give you some words of wisdom for the new year. Mutual satisfaction is indicated.

28 You will have to transform your residence, because a group of friends and relatives may unexpectedly arrive. So much for your relaxing holiday!

29 You could be focusing on what you didn't achieve this year, rather than looking at the positive outcomes of what you did achieve. Look at the cup as being half full.

30 You feel a revival of friendship just now, and are intense about taking partnerships to a new level. You also sense that your friends are in the same mindset.

31 The sextile aspect between the Moon and Jupiter is extremely favourable for the last day of the year. A feeling of fulfilment and connectedness to family and friends underpins your experience.

2012
ASTRONUMEROLOGY

THE BEST THINGS IN LIFE ARE SILLY.

Scott Adams

THE POWER BEHIND
◉ YOUR NAME ◉

It's hard to believe that your name resonates with a numerical vibration, but it's true! Simply by adding together the numbers of your name, you can see which planet rules you and what effects your name will have on your life and destiny. According to the ancient Chaldean system of numerology, each number is assigned a planetary energy, and each alphabetical letter a number, as in the following list:

AIQJY	=	1	**Sun**
BKR	=	2	**Moon**
CGLS	=	3	**Jupiter**
DMT	=	4	**Uranus**
EHNX	=	5	**Mercury**
UVW	=	6	**Venus**
OZ	=	7	**Neptune**
FP	=	8	**Saturn**
—	=	9	**Mars**

Note: The number 9 is not allotted a letter because it was considered 'unknowable'.

Once the numbers have been added, you can establish which single planet rules your name and personal affairs. At this point the number 9 can be used for interpretation. Do you think it's unusual that many famous actors, writers and musicians modify their names? This is to attract luck and good fortune, which can be made easier by using the energies of a friendlier planet. Try experimenting with the table and see how new names affect you. It's so much fun, and you may even attract greater love, wealth and worldly success!

Look at the following example to work out the power of your name. A person named Andrew Brown would calculate his ruling planet by correlating each letter to a number in the table, like this:

A	N	D	R	E	W		B	R	O	W	N
1	5	4	2	5	6		2	2	7	6	5

And then add the numbers like this:

$$1 + 5 + 4 + 2 + 5 + 6 + 2 + 2 + 7 + 6 + 5 \quad = \quad 45$$

Then add

$$4 + 5 \quad = \quad 9$$

The ruling number of Andrew Brown's name is 9, which is governed by Mars (see how the 9 can now be used?). Now study the Name-Number Table to reveal the power of your name. The numbers 4 and 5 will play a secondary role in Andrew's character and destiny, so in his case you would also study the effects of Uranus (4) and Mercury (5).

Name Number	Ruling Planet	Name Characteristics
1	Sun	Attractive personality. Magnetic charm. Superman- or superwoman-like vitality and physical energy. Incredibly active and gregarious. Enjoys outdoor activities and sports. Has friends in powerful positions. Good government connections. Intelligent, spectacular, flashy and successful. A loyal number for love and relationships.
2	Moon	Feminine and soft, with an emotional temperament. Fluctuating moods but intuitive, possibly even has clairvoyant abilities. Ingenious nature. Expresses feelings kind-heartedly. Loves family, motherhood and home life. Night owl who probably needs more sleep. Success with the public and/or women generally.

Name Number	Ruling Planet	Name Characteristics
3	Jupiter	A sociable, optimistic number with a fortunate destiny. Attracts opportunities without too much effort. Great sense of timing. Religious or spiritual inclinations. Naturally drawn to investigating the meaning of life. Philosophical insight. Enjoys travel, explores the world and different cultures.
4	Uranus	Volatile character with many peculiar aspects. Likes to experiment and test novel experiences. Forward-thinking, with many extraordinary friends. Gets bored easily so needs plenty of inspiring activities. Pioneering, technological and creative. Wilful and obstinate at times. Unforeseen events in life may be positive or negative.

Name Number	Ruling Planet	Name Characteristics
5	Mercury	Sharp-witted and quick-thinking, with great powers of speech. Extremely active in life: always on the go and living on nervous energy. Has a youthful outlook and never grows old— looks younger than actual age. Has young friends and a humorous disposition. Loves reading and writing. Great communicator.
6	Venus	Delightful and charming personality. Graceful and eye-catching. Cherishes and nourishes friends. Very active social life. Musical or creative interests. Has great money-making opportunities as well as numerous love affairs. A career in the public eye is quite likely. Loves family, but often troubled over divided loyalties with friends.

Name Number	Ruling Planet	Name Characteristics
7	Neptune	Intuitive, spiritual and self-sacrificing nature. Easily duped by those who need help. Loves to dream of life's possibilities. Has healing powers. Dreams are revealing and prophetic. Loves the water and will have many journeys in life. Spiritual aspirations dominate worldly desires.
8	Saturn	Hard-working, ambitious person with slow yet certain achievements. Remarkable concentration and self-sacrifice for a chosen objective. Financially focused, but generous when a person's trust is gained. Proficient in his or her chosen field but a hard taskmaster. Demands perfection and needs to relax and enjoy life more.

Name Number	Ruling Planet	Name Characteristics
9	Mars	Extraordinary physical drive, desires and ambition. Sports and outdoor activities are major keys to health. Confrontational, but likes to work and play really hard. Protects and defends family, friends and territory. Has individual tastes in life, but is also self-absorbed. Needs to listen to others' advice to gain greater success.

YOUR PLANETARY
◎ RULER ◎

Astrology and numerology are intimately connected. Each planet rules over a number between 1 and 9. Both your name and your birth date are governed by planetary energies. As described earlier, here are the planets and their ruling numbers:

1 **Sun**

2 **Moon**

3 **Jupiter**

4 **Uranus**

5 **Mercury**

6 **Venus**

7 **Neptune**

8 **Saturn**

9 **Mars**

To find out which planet will control the coming year for you, simply add the numbers of your birth date and the year in question. An example follows.

If you were born on 14 November, add the numerals 1 and 4 (14, your day of birth) and 1 and 1 (11, your month of birth) to the year in question, in this case 2012 (current year), like this:

Add 1 + 4 + 1 + 1 + 2 + 0 + 1 + 2   = 12

$$1 + 2 = 3$$

Thus, the planet ruling your individual karma for 2012 would be Jupiter, because this planet rules the number 3.

YOUR PLANETARY
FORECAST ◎

You can even take your ruling name number, as discussed previously, and add it to the year in question to throw more light on your coming personal affairs, like this:

A N D R E W B R O W N	**=**	**9**
Year coming	**=**	**2012**
Add 9 + 2 + 0 + 1 + 2	**=**	**14**
Add 1 + 4	**=**	**5**

Thus, this would be the ruling year number based on your name number. Therefore, you would study the influence of Mercury (5) using the Trends for Your Planetary Number table in 2012. Enjoy!

Trends for Your Planetary Number in 2012

Year Number	Ruling Planet	Results Throughout the Coming Year
1	Sun	**Overview**

Overview

The commencement of a new cycle: a year full of accomplishments, increased reputation and brand new plans and projects.

Many new responsibilities. Success and strong physical vitality. Health should improve and illnesses will be healed.

If you have ailments, now is the time to improve your physical wellbeing—recovery will be certain.

Love and pleasure

A lucky year for love. Creditable connections with children, family life is in focus. Music, art and creative expression will be fulfilling. New romantic opportunities.

Work

Minimal effort for maximum luck. Extra money and exciting opportunities professionally. Positive new changes result in promotion and pay rises.

Improving your luck

Luck is plentiful throughout the year, but especially in July and August. The 1st, 8th, 15th and 22nd hours of Sundays are lucky.

Lucky numbers are 1, 10, 19 and 28.

Year Number	Ruling Planet	Results Throughout the Coming Year
2	Moon	

Overview

Reconnection with your emotions and past. Excellent for relationships with family members. Moodiness may become a problem. Sleeping patterns will be affected.

Love and pleasure

Home, family life and relationships are focused in 2012. Relationships improve through self-effort and greater communication. Residential changes, renovations and interior decoration bring satisfaction. Increased psychic sensitivity.

Work

Emotional in work. Home career, or hobby from a domestic base, will bring greater income opportunities. Females will be more prominent in your work.

Improving your luck

July will fulfil some of your dreams. Mondays will be lucky: the 1st, 8th, 15th and 22nd hours of them are the most fortunate. Pay special attention to the new and full Moons in 2012.

Lucky numbers include 2, 11, 20, 29 and 38.

Year Number	Ruling Planet	Results Throughout the Coming Year
3	Jupiter	

Overview

A lucky year for you. Exciting opportunities arise to expand horizons. Good fortune financially. Travels and increased popularity. A happy year. Spiritual, humanitarian and self-sacrificial focus. Self-improvement is likely.

Love and pleasure

Speculative in love. May meet someone new to travel with, or travel with your friends and lovers. Gambling results in some wins and some losses. Current relationships will deepen in their closeness.

Work

Fortunate for new opportunities and success. Employers are more accommodating and open to your creative expression. Extra money. Promotions are quite possible.

Improving your luck

Remain realistic, get more sleep and don't expect too much from your efforts. Planning is necessary for better luck. The 1st, 8th, 15th and 24th hours of Thursdays are spiritually very lucky for you.

Lucky numbers this year are 3, 12, 21 and 30. March and December are lucky months. The year 2012 will bring some unexpected surprises.

Year Number	Ruling Planet	Results Throughout the Coming Year
4	Uranus	

Overview

Unexpected events, both pleasant and sometimes unpleasant, are likely. Difficult choices appear. Break free of your past and self-imposed limitations. An independent year in which a new path will be forged. Discipline is necessary. Structure your life appropriately, even if doing so is difficult.

Love and pleasure

Guard against dissatisfaction in relationships. Need freedom and experimentation. May meet someone out of the ordinary. Emotional and sexual explorations. Spirituality and community service enhanced. Many new friendships.

Work

Progress is made in work. Technology and other computer or Internet-related industries are fulfilling. Increased knowledge and work skills. New opportunities arise when they are least expected. Excessive work and tension. Learn to relax. Efficiency in time essential. Work with groups and utilise networks to enhance professional prospects.

Year Number	Ruling Planet	Results Throughout the Coming Year
		Improving your luck

Moderation is the key word. Be patient and do not rush things. Slow your pace this year, as being impulsive will only lead to errors and missed opportunities. Exercise greater patience in all matters. Steady investments are lucky.

The 1st, 8th, 15th and 20th hours of any Saturday will be very lucky in 2012.

Your lucky numbers are 4, 13, 22 and 31.

Year Number	Ruling Planet	Results Throughout the Coming Year
5	Mercury	**Overview**

Overview

Intellectual activities and communication increases. Imagination is powerful. Novel and exciting new concepts will bring success and personal satisfaction.

Goal-setting will be difficult. Acquire the correct information before making decisions. Develop concentration and stay away from distracting or negative people.

Love and pleasure

Give as much as you take in relationships. Changes in routine are necessary to keep your love life upbeat and progressive. Develop open-mindedness.

Avoid being critical of your partner. Keep your opinions to yourself. Artistic pursuits and self-improvement are factors in your relationships.

Work

Become a leader in your field in 2012. Contracts, new job offers and other agreements open up new pathways to success. Develop business skills.

Speed, efficiency and capability are your key words this year. Don't be impulsive in making any career changes. Travel is also on the agenda.

Year Number	Ruling Planet	Results Throughout the Coming Year
		Improving your luck

Write ideas down, research topics more thoroughly, communicate enthusiasm through meetings—this will afford you much more luck. Stick to one idea.

The 1st, 8th, 15th and 20th hours of Wednesdays are luckiest, so schedule meetings and other important social engagements at these times.

Throughout 2012 your lucky numbers are 5, 14, 23 and 32.

Year Number	Ruling Planet	Results Throughout the Coming Year
6	Venus	

Overview

A year of love. Expect romantic and sensual interludes, and new love affairs. Number 6 is also related to family life. Working with a loved one or family member is possible, with good results. Save money, cut costs. Share success.

Love and pleasure

The key word for 2012 is romance. Current relationships are deepened. New relationships will be formed and may have some karmic significance, especially if single. Spend time grooming and beautifying yourself: put your best foot forward. Engagement and even marriage is possible. Increased social responsibilities. Moderate excessive tendencies.

Work

Further interest in financial matters and future material security. Reduce costs and become frugal. Extra cash is likely. Additional income or bonuses are possible. Working from home may also be of interest. Social activities and work coincide.

Year Number	Ruling Planet	Results Throughout the Coming Year

Improving your luck

Work and success depend on a creative and positive mental attitude. Eliminate bad habits and personal tendencies that are obstructive. Balance spiritual and financial needs.

The 1st, 8th, 15th and 20th hours on Fridays are extremely lucky this year, and new opportunities can arise when they are least expected.

The numbers 6, 15, 24 and 33 will generally increase your luck.

Year Number	Ruling Planet	Results Throughout the Coming Year
7	Neptune	**Overview**

Overview

An intuitive and spiritual year. Your life path becomes clear. Focus on your inner powers to gain a greater understanding and perspective of your true mission in life. Remove emotional baggage. Make peace with past lovers who have hurt or betrayed you. Forgiveness is the key word this year.

Love and pleasure

Spend time loving yourself, not just bending over backwards for others. Sacrifice to those who are worthy. Relationships should be reciprocal. Avoid deception, swindling or other forms of gossip. Affirm what you want in a relationship to your lover. Set high standards.

Work

Unselfish work is the key to success. Learn to say no to demanding employers or co-workers. Remove clutter to make space for bigger and better things. Healing and caring professions may feature strongly. Use your intuition to manoeuvre carefully into new professional directions.

Year Number	Ruling Planet	Results Throughout the Coming Year

Improving your luck

Maintain cohesive lines of communication and stick to one path for best results. Pay attention to health and don't let stress affect a positive outlook. Sleep well, exercise and develop better eating habits to improve energy circulation.

The 1st, 8th, 15th and 20th hours of Wednesdays are luckiest, so schedule meetings and other important social engagements at these times.

Throughout 2012 your lucky numbers are 7, 16, 25 and 34.

Year Number	Ruling Planet	Results Throughout the Coming Year
8	Saturn	

Overview

This is a practical year requiring effort, hard work and a certain amount of solitude for best results. Pay attention to structure, timelines and your diary. Don't try to help too many people, but rather, focus on yourself. This will be a year of discipline and self-analysis. However, income levels will eventually increase.

Love and pleasure

Balance personal affairs with work. Show affection to loved ones through practicality and responsibility.

Dedicate time to family, not just work. Schedule activities outdoors for increased wellbeing and emotional satisfaction.

Work

Money is on the increase this year, but continued focus is necessary. Hard work equals extra income. A cautious and resourceful year, but be generous where possible. Some new responsibilities will bring success. Balance income potential with creative satisfaction.

Year Number	Ruling Planet	Results Throughout the Coming Year

Improving your luck

Being overcautious and reluctant to attempt something new will cause delay and frustration if new opportunities are offered. Be kind to yourself and don't overwork or overdo exercise. Send out positive thought-waves to friends and loved ones. The karmic energy will return.

The 1st, 8th, 15th and 20th hours of Saturdays are the best times for you in 2012.

The numbers 1, 8, 17, 26 and 35 are lucky.

Year Number	Ruling Planet	Results Throughout the Coming Year
9	Mars	

Overview

The ending of one chapter of your life and the preparation for the beginning of a new cycle. A transition period when things may be in turmoil or a state of uncertainty. Remain calm. Do not be impulsive or irritable. Avoid arguments. Calm communication will help find solutions.

Love and pleasure

Tremendous energy and drive help you achieve goals this year. But don't be too pushy when forcing your ideas down other people's throats, so to speak. Diplomatic discussions, rather than arguments, should be used to achieve outcomes. Discuss changes before making decisions with partners and lovers in your life.

Work

A successful year with the expectation of bigger and better things next year. Driven by work objectives or ambition. Tendency to overdo and overwork. Pace your deadlines. Leadership role likely. Respect and honour from your peers and employers.

Year Number	Ruling Planet	Results Throughout the Coming Year
		Improving your luck

Find adequate outlets for your high level of energy through meditation, self-reflection and prayer. Collect your energies and focus them on one point. Release tension to maintain health.

The 1st, 8th, 15th and 20th hours of Tuesdays will be lucky for you throughout 2012.

Your lucky numbers are 9, 18, 27 and 36.

The World of Mills & Boon®

There's a Mills & Boon® series that's perfect for you. We publish ten series and with new titles every month, you never have to wait long for your favourite to come along.

Blaze® — Scorching hot, sexy reads

By Request — Relive the romance with the best of the best

Cherish™ — Romance to melt the heart every time

Desire™ — Passionate and dramatic love stories

Visit us Online — Browse our books before you buy online at **www.millsandboon.co.uk**

M&B/WORLD